Between the Laws of God and Man

Between the Laws of God and Man

Punishment and Forgiveness in American and Biblical Jewish Law

REUVEN TRAVIS

Foreword by Michael J. Broyde

WIPF & STOCK · Eugene, Oregon

BETWEEN THE LAWS OF GOD AND MAN
Punishment and Forgiveness in American and Biblical Jewish Law

Copyright © 2024 Reuven Travis. All rights reserved. Except for brief quotations in critical publications or reviews, no part of this book may be reproduced in any manner without prior written permission from the publisher. Write: Permissions, Wipf and Stock Publishers, 199 W. 8th Ave., Suite 3, Eugene, OR 97401.

Wipf & Stock
An Imprint of Wipf and Stock Publishers
199 W. 8th Ave., Suite 3
Eugene, OR 97401

www.wipfandstock.com

PAPERBACK ISBN: 979-8-3852-2137-0
HARDCOVER ISBN: 979-8-3852-2138-7
EBOOK ISBN: 979-8-3852-2139-4

VERSION NUMBER 091924

In memory of my parents

LARRY AND INA TRAVIS

who thought, and perhaps even hoped,
that someday I might become a lawyer.

I may not have practiced law, but at least now I have written about it.

"No man is above the law and no man is below it: nor do we ask any man's permission when we ask him to obey it."
—Theodore Roosevelt

"If we were all righteous, we should need no law or torts."
—Rabbi Avraham ibn Ezra

Contents

Acknowledgments | ix
Foreword by Michael J. Broyde | xi

CHAPTER ONE
Introduction | 1

CHAPTER TWO
The Purpose of Law | 6

CHAPTER THREE
Different Notions of Foundational Texts | 25

CHAPTER FOUR
Underlying Expectations | 46

CHAPTER FIVE
Case Studies | 61

CHAPTER SIX
Final Thoughts | 98

Bibliography | 105

Acknowledgments

THE GENESIS OF THIS book are the many conversations I have had with my rabbi and teacher Michael J. Broyde on the continued relevance of the Torah for contemporary America. To date, I have been privileged to co-author three books with Rabbi Broyde on this topic,[1] and it is our plan to write two others. For me, this book represents a logical continuation of our collaborative endeavors.

I also want to thank my wife Laura Kahn for her many suggestions that in the end made this a much better book than it might otherwise have been.

Unless otherwise indicated, all translations of biblical verses in this book are taken from *Tanakh: A New Translation of the Holy Scriptures according to the Traditional Hebrew Text*, which appears on Sefaria (Sefaria.org). This translation is available in the public domain and with a free public license thanks to Sefaria.

ABOUT THE AUTHOR

Prior to his career as an educator, Rabbi Reuven Travis spent fifteen years as a consultant, as well as an advertising and marketing executive. He then changed professions and started his career as an educator. He has taught a wide range of classes, including courses on Jewish law, Bible, Jewish history, Zionism, the Shoah, Israel advocacy, American history and civics, and African American history.

Rabbi Travis earned his bachelor's degree from Dartmouth College, where he graduated Phi Beta Kappa. He holds an additional master's degree

---

1. Broyde and Travis, *Sex in the Garden*; *Finding America in Exodus*; and *Finding America In Leviticus*.

in teaching from Mercer University and a master's degree in Judaic studies from Spertus College. He received his rabbinic ordination in 2006 from Rabbi Michael J. Broyde, dean of the Atlanta Torah MiTzion Kollel, after spending four years studying with members of the kollel.

Rabbi Travis has collaborated with Rabbi Broyde on books that demonstrate the relevance of Genesis, Exodus, and Leviticus for America in the twenty-first century. Rabbi Travis separately published three scholarly works on the book of Job, the book of Numbers, and the book of Genesis, respectively. He also authored a series of books about the weekly parasha for parents and educators of third, fourth, and fifth grade children.

Foreword

IT IS WITH GREAT pleasure that I introduce Reuven Travis's profound work, *Between the Laws of God and Man: Punishment and Forgiveness in American and Biblical Jewish Law*. This book explores the intricate dance between secular and religious legal systems, focusing on the pivotal themes of punishment and forgiveness.

Reuven Travis presents a scholarly yet accessible examination of how American legal principles and Biblical Jewish law intersect and diverge. Through thoughtful analysis and comparative case studies, he illuminates how these two legal traditions address human transgression and mercy. This exploration is particularly relevant in our contemporary context, where questions of justice and compassion are at the forefront of public discourse.

As a scholar deeply invested in both secular and religious jurisprudence, I find Travis's work to be an invaluable contribution to the field. His ability to draw connections between ancient texts and modern legal practices provides readers with a deeper understanding of the values underpinning our legal systems and the connections between secular and religious law, no matter what one's faith.

This book is a resource not only for legal scholars but also for anyone interested in the moral and ethical dimensions of law. I am confident that readers will find Travis's insights both enlightening and thought-provoking.

—Michael J. Broyde
Professor of law at Emory University School of Law, the director of the SJD Program, and Berman Projects Director at the Center for the Study of Law and Religion at Emory University

CHAPTER ONE

Introduction

AT FIRST GLANCE, ONE of the main pillars of Jewish law is hard to understand. It is in the Talmud where this extraordinary ruling is rendered: *dina de-malchuta dina*, that is, "the law of the kingdom is the law."[1] Some have called this "one of the most famous, far-reaching and even revolutionary laws of the Talmud."[2]

What's going on here? Why would Jewish law defer to secular law? Under what circumstances would it do so?

Most people, be they Jew or Gentile, are likely to associate Jewish law with ritual matters, and with good reason. The Talmud, the great compendium of Jewish law, is replete with intricate discussions on a wide variety of ritual matters. For instance, there is an entire tractate (among the longest in the Talmud) devoted to the laws of the Sabbath. Another deals almost exclusively with the Paschal sacrifice that was brought in Temple times during the Passover festival and the laws of the seder held annually by Jews around the world. There are tractates on Rosh Hashanah (the Jewish New Year), Yom Kippur (the Day of Atonement), the festival of Tabernacles (Sukkot in Hebrew), and the Purim holiday. There is a tractate that discusses what objects can be used during these festivals, which labors are permitted on such days, and how food can be prepared. There is even one that covers the sacrifices that were brought to the Temple in Jerusalem on the three

---

1. This principle is cited four times in the Talmud (Nedarim 28a; Gittin 10b; Bava Kamma 113a; Bava Batra 54b and 55a).
2. Kellman, "The Law of the Land: Bava Kamma 113."

Between the Laws of God and Man

biblically ordained pilgrimage festivals and the degree of ritual purity required to bring such sacrifices.[3]

Yet, *halakha* (the Hebrew term generally used meaning "Jewish law") is not limited to ritual matters, and, as will be evident in the following chapters, the Talmud itself is far more than a compilation of ritual requirements and practices. It also reads very much like a legal text and has many parallels to secular law. Given this, why would the Talmudic sages institute this notion of *dina de-malchuta dina*?

The Talmud provides no legal basis for this principle. Moreover, the first generation of post-Talmudic sages, the *Geonim*, are mostly silent on this topic.[4] One responsum from the geonic period suggests that *dina de-malchuta dina* was instituted for practical religious reasons. The responsum acknowledges the realities of the era, namely, that Jews were living under the rule of a foreign government, and posits that it is the will of God that Jews should obey the laws of their rulers.[5] Among the later explanations put forth for *dina de-malchuta dina* was the idea that Jewish law can, in certain cases, accept non-Jewish law because non-Jews are commanded to enact laws to preserve orderly social life.[6]

Whatever the rationale for *dina de-malchuta dina* is, it does seem that it effectively renders much of Jewish law inoperative, only to be replaced by the laws of the country within which Jews live. One simple example illustrates this point. The Torah requires a worker be paid every day. Yet, Jewish employees at Jewish organizations are paid much less often in accordance with the prevailing commercial practice in the United States, be it on a monthly or bi-monthly or perhaps weekly basis. To pay them on a different schedule from their Gentile co-workers would be practically impossible and perhaps morally indefensible.[7]

The notion of living lives governed by two distinct (and sometimes conflicting) legal systems—*halakha* and the laws governing the lands of their exiles—is nothing new for the Jewish people. After all, they have been doing this since the destruction of the Second Temple by the Romans in 70

---

3. Passover, Pentecost (Shavuot in Hebrew), and Sukkot.

4. The *Geonim* were the heads of the ancient talmudic academies of Babylonia. They gained ascendancy over the older Palestinian center of Judaism and were recognized as the leading religious and spiritual authorities by most of the world's Jewish population. Brody, *The Geonim of Babylonia and the Shaping of Medieval Jewish Culture*.

5. Assaf, *Teshuvot ha-Ge'onim*, no. 66.

6. "Dina De-Malkhuta Dina."

7. Kellman, "The Law of the Land: Bava Kamma 113."

Introduction

CE. Today is no different, notwithstanding the reestablishment of Jewish sovereignty over Israel in 1948. The majority of Jews in the world continue to live in "exile," far from the land of Israel and the legal system intended to maintain its identity as a Jewish state.[8] For Jews living in western democracies, this typically means balancing the demands of *halakha* with secular law. Indeed, according to Chaim Saiman, "throughout their history, Jews have been subject to political and legal systems that compete with *halakha*, and to which *halakha* has often accommodated itself." [9]

The average Jew living in America rarely feels any tension between secular and Jewish law. For example, before American Jews get married under a chuppah, they obtain a marriage license from the state. They celebrate many rituals surrounding the birth of a child and obtain a birth certificate from the state and a social security number for the child from the federal government. They are likely to give to a variety of charities and do so while also paying their state and federal taxes. They purchase homes and apply for mortgages in accordance with state laws, not *halakha*.

As an Orthodox Jew and a proud American, I, too, have long lived this simultaneous existence without pondering how one of my legal points of reference affects the other. That changed over the past several years, as I have been working on a series of books that examine the relevance of the Torah for contemporary America. These books, in part, focused on the legal systems of the United States and of Judaism and on which values they share and where their approaches to law differ. The more I pondered this, the more I realized that my work in these books only scratched the surface. This, in turn, motivated me to delve deeper into this idea and persuaded me to write this book.

Full transparency is in order. I am not a lawyer although, I have availed myself to some wonderful legal resources, especially that of Michael J. Broyde, my mentor and a professor of law at Emory University School of Law.[10] I am an educator and a rabbi who has taught Jewish law and his-

---

8. According to the Jewish Agency for Israel, as of September 2022, approximately 54 percent of world Jewry lives outside of Israel. "Jewish Population Rises to 15.3 Million Worldwide, with 7 Million Residing in Israel."

9. Saiman, *Halakhah*, 9.

10. Among the many helpful insights I gleaned from his lectures and writings, one in particular caught my attention: "In Jewish law, the core value is legal duty. In modern-day America the coin of the realm is rights." Broyde, *Contrasts in American and Jewish Law*, xxiii. Broyde further suggests that the secular tradition will often create rights without duties, whereas the Jewish tradition frequently comes close to creating duties without

tory as well as American history and civics for many years. My discussions of secular law will therefore be those of a layperson, and the comparative analyses of both Jewish and secular law, notwithstanding the details and nuances I bring to bear, are intended neither for lawyers nor for Jewish scholars.

With this in mind, my goal is to explore key core elements of Jewish and secular law to determine commonalities, divergences, and implications of each as follows:

- First, I will examine the purpose of each and demonstrate how the very different starting points for Jewish and secular law drive each in very different directions, in particular when it comes down to matters of what is "right" versus what is "legal."
- Second, I will explore how the foundational documents of each code developed and continue to develop, which then delineates the flexibility and rigidity of both legal systems.
- Third, I want to consider the underlying expectations and desired outcomes of each and specifically contrast the optimism I believe is inherent in Jewish law (with its hope that sinners can and will repent) with the relative pessimism I see in the American legal system (which seems, at least to me, to embrace the idea of "once a criminal, always a criminal").

This is surely not the only way to think about this complicated and complex topic, but in addressing these points, my hope is that readers of this book who have an interest in the worlds of Jewish and American law will end up with a greater appreciation of how each informs and directs the other.

---

rights. He illustrates this point via a comparison of the modern right to an education with the ancient Jewish version of it. Before 1960 only two states embraced education as a fundamental right: Wyoming and North Carolina. In 1960, Maryland added education to its Declaration of Rights. Then, in 1976, the California Supreme Court held in Serrano v. Priest (1976), held that education is a fundamental right under the state's constitution. Courts in Connecticut, Washington, and West Virginia soon followed suit. Mississippi, Oklahoma, Wisconsin, and Kentucky recognized the right to a quality education under their state constitutions in the 1980s. In contrast, Jewish law never speaks of a right to an education, but rather the duty incumbent upon parents, and, in their absence or inability to do so, the community, to educate children. Moreover, should a child not receive an education, Jewish law imposed a duty on this individual upon reaching adulthood to pursue one. The difference between rights and duties will figure prominently in the case studies set forth later in this book.

Introduction

One stylistic note. This book is heavily footnoted. And this is not because the footnotes are essential for following the flow of my arguments. They are not. Rather, they reflect my many years as an educator, when I always strove to provide my students with a context for the material we were discussing. The footnotes in this book do precisely that: they provide a general background that will help put matters into context. The footnotes are also there to define Hebrew terms and legal concepts. Whether you read the footnotes or skip them entirely, you will have a better understanding of the interaction of Jewish and American law when you reach the end of this book.

CHAPTER TWO

The Purpose of Law

THE PURPOSE OF SECULAR LAW

As we begin our examination of Jewish and secular law, we need to pose the most basic question—that is, "what is the purpose of the law?"—because it reflects the most axiomatic difference between the two legal systems.

Philosophers and scholars have pondered the question of the purpose of law for centuries. As H. L. A. Hart, a much-respected professor of jurisprudence at Oxford University, observed, "few questions concerning human society have been asked with such persistence and answered by serious thinkers in so many diverse, strange and even paradoxical ways."[1] Writing in the thirteenth century, Thomas Aquinas suggested that law is "an ordinance of reason for the common good" put forward by those who have "care of the community."[2] Some three hundred years later, John Locke argued that the law is not meant to abolish or restrain freedom, but rather to preserve and enlarge it. In his view, "in all the states of created beings capable of law, where there is no law, there is no freedom."[3]

---

1. Mbewe, "The role of law," 84.

2. Thomas Aquinas, an Italian Dominican friar and priest, was an influential philosopher and theologian. He was also a jurist in the tradition of scholasticism. He produced a comprehensive synthesis of Christian theology and Aristotelian philosophy that influenced Roman Catholic doctrine for centuries. Aquinas, *Summa Theologica*, Questions 90–97.

3. John Locke was an English philosopher and physician, widely regarded as one of the most influential of Enlightenment thinkers and commonly known as the "father of liberalism." Locke, *Second Treatise on Civil Government*, chapter 6, section 57.

The Purpose of Law

In matters such as these, Americans are fond of turning to the country's founders for their thoughts and perspectives, and Thomas Jefferson is among the most quoted of this group. He was greatly influenced by the writings of Locke, but his focus was more on the individual than was Locke's and his attitude vis-à-vis the law far more pessimistic. Jefferson maintained that:

> Rightful liberty is unobstructed action according to our will within limits drawn around us by the equal rights of others. I do not add 'within the limits of the law' because law is often but the tyrant's will, and always so when it violates the rights of the individual.[4]

From my perspective, I believe Justice Joseph Bradley, who served as an associate justice of the Supreme Court from 1870 to 1892, and his description of the purpose of the law. I think he summed it up best when he said, "Society cannot exist without law. Law is the bond of society: that which makes it, that which preserves it and keeps it together. It is, in fact, the essence of civil society."[5]

Such quotes and observations may be insightful and perhaps even inspiring. Yet, upon reflection, they really do not give us a practical answer to our question. Let us therefore start again with the basics.

Black's Law Dictionary defines law as "a body of rules of action or conduct prescribed by a controlling authority and having binding legal force. That which must be obeyed and followed by citizens subject to sanctions or legal consequence is a law."[6]

Leave it to a law dictionary to make even a simple definition sound complicated.

In simpler parlance, laws are rules that bind all people living in a community. Laws protect our general safety and ensure our rights as citizens against abuses by other people, by organizations, and by the government itself. In short, "the law is a system that governs social behavior within a given political community."[7]

The law thus sets forth a framework for minimally acceptable behavior, not from a social or cultural perspective but rather on a criminal basis. Criminal activities are deemed so because society (through a legislative

---

4. "Letter from Thomas Jefferson to Isaac H. Tiffany."
5. Bradley "Law, Its Nature and Office as the Bond and Basis of Civil Society."
6. Black's Law Dictionary, 6th ed., s.v. "law."
7. Saiman, *Halakhah*, 29.

body) has determined that it will not tolerate certain behaviors that injure or damage persons or their property.

At its most basic level, the law is meant to restrict or curb unacceptable (in the sense of harmful or destructive) behaviors. It is, in a word, about constraint, and this translates into three critical governance roles:

- First, it is through law and legal institutions that states seek to *order the behavior* of individuals and organizations so economic and social policies are converted into outcomes.
- Second, law defines the structure of government by *ordering power*—that is, establishing and distributing authority and power among government actors and between the state and citizens.
- And third, law also serves to *order contestation* by providing the substantive and procedural tools needed to promote accountability, resolve disputes peacefully, and change the rules.[8]

Regardless of whether the law is the command of the state, an expression of values and ideas ingrained in human nature, or social convention, the definition of law coalesces around a central case: a system of governance residing in a political community where there is a reasonable possibility that the law will be enforced.[9] It is precisely this possibility that leads individuals to adhere to the law.

In a perfect world, individuals obey the law without coercion, along the lines of Locke's theory of the social contract. In the second of his *Two Treatises of Government*, Locke envisions the state of nature as one in which humans, though free, equal, and independent, are obliged under the law of nature to respect each other's rights to life, liberty, and property.[10] Yet, disputes inevitably arise, and injuries inevitably require redress. Individuals therefore agree to form a commonwealth (and thereby to leave the state of nature) in order to institute an impartial power capable of arbitrating such matters. For Locke, the obligation to obey civil government under the social contract was conditional upon the protection of the natural rights of each person, including the right to private property.[11]

---

8. Mbewe, "The role of law," 83.
9. Saiman, *Halakhah*, 30.
10. Locke, *Two Treatises of Government*. Phoenix.
11. Friend, "Social Contract Theory."

The Purpose of Law

While most societies embrace some form of Locke's social contract, compliance by individuals with the demands of their civil government is often driven by the coercive power of law, which in turn depends on the existence of a credible threat of being caught and punished or a credible commitment to obtaining a reward for compliance.[12] In other words, the law must provide incentives that are strong enough to overcome the gains from noncompliance while taking into account the fact that many people may not exhibit "rational behavior." These "incentives" must also be strong enough to overcome adherence to any alternative conflicting normative order.

What we see, then, is that a functioning legal system needs both law and sufficient incentives to induce rational compliance among the members of society; this marks the fundamental starting point for secular law.

In the United States, these incentives are punishment-based and encompass a wide range of consequences, including fines, imprisonment, community service, and probation. On the most basic level, they serve as a deterrent to criminal behaviors, since people are less likely to break the law if they know they will face consequences. They also provide a means of holding criminals accountable for their actions while ensuring that they are punished for the harm they cause.

Given that serious consequences result from illegal activities, individuals are logically motivated to ask a very simple question: is it legal or not? For many, if not most individuals, there is no other question to be asked. Whether a given action is "right" or "just" frequently pales in comparison to the legality of the action. An unjust action may weigh on the conscience of the individual, but who among us would consider pangs of conscience to be a serious consequence?

This deference of justice in the face of legality is supported by the founding document of the American legal system: the US Constitution. Quite simply, the Constitution "does not aim to instruct people on the virtues, or the content of happiness, or the path to salvation."[13] Not because virtue is irrelevant or because happiness has no content. Rather, as Peter Berkowitz frames it, the Constitution presupposes that the people, as individuals and through the various associations and groups they form, will

---

12. Mbewe, "The role of law," 86. As Mbewe further notes: "That credibility depends on the extent to which the law is able to coordinate people's beliefs and expectations about what others—fellow citizens and the officials who implement and enforce laws—will do."

13. Berkowitz, "The Court."

pursue good.[14] In recognition of this, the Constitution establishes a framework for how American citizens can maintain a society where each "has the liberty to pursue, consistent with a like liberty for others, virtue, happiness, and salvation in the way each regards as fitting."[15]

Said differently, the Constitution defines what is legal, not what is moral. In fact, some argue that there is an inverse relationship between legality and morality in American law. Grant Gilmore, one of the twentieth century's best-known law professors and co-author of the Uniform Commercial Code, sums up this perspective quite nicely when he wrote that "the better the society, the less law there will be. In heaven there will be no law . . . The worse the society, the more law there will be. In hell there will be nothing but law, and due process will be meticulously observed."[16]

This disconnect between morality and legality is exemplified by what is arguably the most sweeping and influential ruling by the US Supreme Court in the twentieth century. Understanding the significance of this decision requires a bit of background.

During the Reconstruction era (1865–1900), the political rights of Black Americans were affirmed by three constitutional amendments and numerous laws passed by Congress, most notably by the Civil Rights Act of 1875. This legislation made it a crime for an individual to deny "the full and equal enjoyment of any of the accommodations, advantages, facilities, and privileges of inns, public conveyances on land or water, theaters and other places of public amusement; subject only to the conditions and limitations established by law, and applicable alike to citizens of every race and color."[17]

The protections against racial discrimination established by this 1875 act were ultimately overturned by the Supreme Court in two landmark decisions. The first, issued in 1883, ruled that the Fourteenth Amendment did not give Congress authority to prevent discrimination by private individuals. Instead, the Court ruled that victims of racial discrimination should seek relief from the states, not from the federal government.[18]

The second was decided in 1896. In a case that strikes modern readers as both incomprehensible and immoral, the Supreme Court upheld a Louisiana state law that allowed for "equal but separate accommodations for

14. Berkowitz, "The Court."
15. Berkowitz, "The Court."
16. Gilmore, *The Ages of American Law*, 110.
17. *Plessy v. Ferguson*, 163 U.S. 537 (1896).
18. *Civil Rights Cases*, 109 U.S. 3 (1883).

The Purpose of Law

the white and colored races" in railroad passenger coaches in Louisiana.[19] Segregation in most public and semi-public facilities, the result of the "Jim Crow" laws, was thus deemed to be legal throughout the United States.

This shameful era finally came to end when, in 1954, the Supreme Court unanimously ruled that state-sanctioned segregation of public schools was a violation of the 14th amendment and was therefore unconstitutional.[20] This historic decision marked the end of the "separate but equal" precedent set by the Supreme Court nearly sixty years earlier in *Plessy v. Ferguson* and served as a catalyst for the expanding civil rights movement during the decade of the 1950s.[21]

It also is informative to consider the language of the *Brown v. Board of Education of Topeka* decision:

> Segregation of white and Negro children in the public schools of a State solely on the basis of race, pursuant to state laws permitting or requiring such segregation, denies to Negro children the equal protection of the laws guaranteed by the Fourteenth Amendment—even though the physical facilities and other "tangible" factors of white and Negro schools may be equal.

(a) The history of the Fourteenth Amendment is inconclusive as to its intended effect on public education.

(b) The question presented in these cases must be determined not on the basis of conditions existing when the Fourteenth Amendment was adopted, but in the light of the full development of public education and its present place in American life throughout the Nation.

(c) Where a State has undertaken to provide an opportunity for an education in its public schools, such an opportunity is a right which must be made available to all on equal terms.

(d) Segregation of children in public schools solely on the basis of race deprives children of the minority group of equal educational

---

19. *Plessy v. Ferguson*, 163 U.S. 537 (1896). On at least six occasions over nearly sixty years, the Supreme Court held, either explicitly or by necessary implication, that the "separate but equal" rule announced in Plessy was the correct rule of law. *Cumming v. Board of Education*, 175 U.S. 528 (1899); *Berea College v. Kentucky*, 211 U.S. 45 (1908); *Gong Lum v. Rice*, 275 U.S. 78 (1927); *Missouri ex rel. Gaines v. Canada*, 305 U.S. 337 (1938); *Sipuel v. Board of Regents*, 332 U.S. 631 (1948); *Sweatt v. Painter*, 339 U.S. 629 (1950).

20. *Brown v. Board of Education of Topeka*, 347 U.S. 483 (1954).

21. *Plessy v. Ferguson*, 163 U.S. 537 (1896).

opportunities, even though the physical facilities and other "tangible" factors may be equal.

(e) The "separate but equal" doctrine adopted in *Plessy v. Ferguson*, 163 U.S. 537, has no place in the field of public education.

The Court here did what one should expect from its decisions. No sermonizing about the degradations and humiliations suffered by Blacks and other people of color during the Jim Crow era. No sense of moral outrage. No righteous judgements. Only cold, clear legal rationale, namely, that segregation of children in public schools solely because of their race deprives children of the minority group of equal educational opportunities and that this violates the "Equal Protection Clause" of the Fourteenth Amendment.[22]

The inapplicability of moral standards when deciding matters of law was explicitly broached in a recent holding by the Ninth Circuit United States Court of Appeals.[23] The three-judge panel for the circuit court concluded in a published opinion that a Spanish state-controlled museum is the proper owner of the painting, "Rue Saint-Honoré, après-midi, effet de pluie," a nineteenth century work by Danish-French (and Jewish) impressionist Camille Pissarro said to be worth tens of millions of dollars. The panel concluded in its decision that the museum had gained prescriptive title to the painting under Spanish law since it had purchased the work without knowing that the Nazis had stolen it from a Jewish family and that the museum had held it long enough to gain title through possession. US Circuit Judge Consuelo M. Callahan wrote in a concurrence that while she agreed with the result under the law, she was nevertheless troubled by it. Callahan wrote:

> Spain, having reaffirmed its commitment to the Washington Principles on Nazi-Confiscate[d] Art when it signed the Terezin Declaration on Holocaust Era Assets and Related Issues, should have voluntarily relinquished the painting, However, as we previously held, "we cannot order compliance with the Washington Principles or the Terezin Declaration." Our opinion is compelled

---

22. Section 1 of the Fourteenth Amendment states that "No State shall make or enforce any law which shall abridge the privileges or immunities of citizens of the United States; nor shall any State deprive any person of life, liberty, or property, without due process of law; nor deny to any person within its jurisdiction the equal protection of the laws."

23. *Cassirer v. Thyssen Bornemisza Collection Foundation*, 69 F.4th 554, 564. (9th Cir. 2023).

The Purpose of Law

by the district court's findings of fact and the applicable law, but I wish that it were otherwise.

Simply put, while Judge Callahan believed the museum had a moral duty to return the painting to the California man who filed the case nearly two decades ago—David Cassirer, the great-grandson of Holocaust survivor Lilly Neubauer, from whom the painting had been stolen as she was fleeing Germany in 1939—she concurred with her colleagues that the law could not require its return. This is a classic example where "what is legal" takes precedence over "what is right."

The lack of consideration of the morality when deciding these and other such cases does not mean that the concept of justice has no place in American law. Indeed, the line between justice and the law can be subjective, and many people frequently misunderstand and conflate the two. Complicating matters even more is the lack of a single definition of justice:

> Social justice is the notion that everyone deserves equal economic, political, and social opportunities irrespective of race, gender, or religion. Distributive justice refers to the equitable allocation of assets in society. Environmental justice is the fair treatment of all people with regard to environmental burdens and benefits. Restorative or corrective justice seeks to make whole those who have suffered unfairly. Retributive justice seeks to punish wrongdoers objectively and proportionately. And procedural justice refers to implementing legal decisions in accordance with fair and unbiased processes.[24]

The significance of each of these standards of justice is based on one's cultural, historical, and individual perspectives. Ideally, true justice would align with the spirit of the law and the principles of fairness, equity, and human rights. Sadly, however, this is not always the case, and achieving a balance between the two is often a matter of ongoing debate and interpretation. What is generally not a matter of debate is the legality of particular acts. Robbery, assault, embezzlement, and even murder can be justified (and frequently is) by the perpetrators of such crimes. If and when these perpetrators stand trial, they do not argue that their actions were legal. They instead maintain that they are innocent of the charges brought against them, sometimes based on facts and other times based on technical parsings of the law.

24. "Justice."

Between the Laws of God and Man

THE PURPOSE OF JEWISH LAW

Most people tend to associate Jewish law with ritual matters and thus would not be surprised to learn that the Talmud opens with a Jew's obligation to recite a core prayer declaring the unity of God, the *Shema*, twice daily. Less expected, however, is the fact that the Talmud is also a legal text as we commonly think of the term. In the tractate entitled Sanhedrin, we find the details of the judicial system that was in place prior to the destruction of the Temple and the exile of the Jewish people, including how the courts were formed, how and when testimony was accepted by the courts, and how and when capital punishment could be administered. More telling are the "Three Gates"—the tractates of Bava Kamma, Bava Metzia, and Bava Batra—which contain a complex and very detailed system of torts.[25] Specifically, Bava Kamma focuses on the laws of damages, Bava Metzia on commercial dealings, and Bava Batra on property rights.

For all the preponderance of ritual matters found in the Talmud, the sages recognized the importance and value of studying what we would call civil law: "Rabbi Yishmael said: One who wants to become wise should engage in [the study of] monetary law, as there is no greater discipline in the Torah, and it is like a flowing spring."[26] Modern law school students would likely agree with this sentiment, as the discussions and theoretical cases set forth in the "Three Gates" seem to echo those found in standard law school text books.

Consider some of cases examined in the first gate, Bava Kamma. A person who digs a pit or places an obstacle in a public thoroughfare is liable for damages incurred by people and animals that fall in the pit or trip on the obstacle. However, the individual can avoid liability by covering the pit. But, what happens if the cover is damaged from below, either by moisture or insects? Must the person have had inspected the cover on both sides to avoid liability?

What if this person constructed a cover strong enough to bear the weight of an ox, but not that of a camel? Should a camel walk on the cover, thereby weakening it, so that it collapses under the weight of an ox which later passes by, is the pit owner liable or not? If camels are not common

---

25. A tort is an act or omission that gives rise to injury or harm to another and amounts to a civil wrong for which courts impose liability. In the context of torts, "injury" describes the invasion of any legal right, whereas "harm" describes a loss or detriment in fact that an individual suffers. "Tort."

26. Mishna Bava Batra 10:8.

to the area, must the cover nonetheless be strong enough to support their weight?

What if the pit is owned by two people? Is there shared liability? What if one person dug most of the pit, and a second person completed it to the depth that incurs liability for damages in Jewish law?[27] Who is liable for the damages? The one who started and dug most of the pit? The one who completed the pit? Both of them?

Clearly, as we get a sense of here, the Talmud is both a religious and a legal code. Yet the religious components of the Talmud deal with more than just ritual matters. It frequently addresses complex moral issues, finding cause to do so based on the verse found in Deuteronomy, which states that the Jewish people are commanded to "Do what is right and good in the sight of the LORD."[28] Among the best-known of the Talmud's discussions related to this is found in a series of cases set forth in Bava Metzia 83a.

The first case examined by the Talmudic sages dealt with issues of liability, or torts as they are called in secular law. In this case, an individual was to buy four hundred barrels of wine. After the purchase, the wine turned sour. Who should bear the cost of the spoiled wine? The one who requested that the purchase be made, or the one who actually made the purchase? The matter was brought before Raba, and he declined to rule on the matter. Instead, he offered advice to the purchaser on how to prove that he was not negligent and thus not liable. Not the behavior one would expect from a rabbi positioned to render a legal decision, but one entirely consistent with the notion of doing that which is "good and right."

By way of contrast, consider the Supreme Court's ruling in *Shinn v. Ramirez* (issued on May 23, 2022). The defendant in this case was sentenced to death for the sexual assault and killing of a four-year-old girl. However, his court-appointed trial court lawyer did not investigate the facts of the case. Arizona law (where the defendant was charged and convicted) does not allow the first post-conviction appeal to raise the question of ineffective assistance of counsel. On the second appeal, the appellate lawyer did not raise the question either. Only when *federal* public defenders were brought into the case for a federal court hearing did they examine the medical evidence and consult experts, who later testified that the injuries inflicted

---

27. Liability is only imposed when the pit is a minimum of ten *tefachim*, which is defined by the Orthodox Union as eighty cm., corresponding to about thirty-two inches. OU Staff, "Tefach."

28. Deuteronomy 6:18.

on the child occurred not when the prosecution claimed, but at a time when Jones was nowhere near the child and could not have inflicted them. Hence, evidence that would have conclusively proven the innocence of the defendant was never considered during his trial and subsequent appeal due to ineffective and inept legal counsel.

A federal appeals court unanimously agreed that the defendant was entitled to a new trial and that this previously undisclosed evidence should be considered. Arizona appealed this ruling, and the Supreme Court held in its favor, despite a 2012 ruling by the court stating that when a state court "substantially" interferes with a defendant's constitutional right to be represented by counsel, the defendant, with a new lawyer, may appeal to federal court to show that he was denied his right to effective counsel. Writing for the majority in the 2022 case, Justice Clarence Thomas said that federal courts may not hear "new evidence" obtained after conviction to show how deficient the trial or appellate lawyer in state court was. To allow such evidence to be presented in federal court, he said, "encourages prisoners to sandbag state courts," depriving the states of "the finality that is essential to both the retributive and deterrent function of criminal law." It seems to me that it would be difficult to find a starker contrast between American and Jewish jurisprudence or between doing "what is legal" versus doing "what is right."

The next case cited in the Talmud is even more telling. In brief, some day-workers were employed by Rabbah bar R. Huna, an individual of significant means. The workers were negligent and broke a barrel of wine. Rabbah bar R. Huna seized their garments as compensation for his loss. The workers in turn went to the sage Rav to complain, who ordered Rabbah bar R. Huna to return the items in question. "Is that the law?" Rabbah bar R. Huna asked. "Even so," Rav replied, "That you may walk in the way of good men" (Tehillim 2:20).

Even though their garments had been returned, the workers had an additional complaint. "We are poor men, have worked all day, and are in need: are we to get nothing?" In response, Rav ordered Rabbah son of R. Huna pay them, despite their negligence and despite his financial loss. "Is that the law?" he asked. "Even so," was Rav's reply, "and keep the path of the righteous" (Tehillim 2:20).

In this case, the rabbi was asked to issue a legal ruling, but instead seems to resort to ethical principles in order to, so to speak, improve upon the law. Rav certainly understood that the employer had a legal right to

The Purpose of Law

seize the garments of his negligent employees. Yet he also knew that following the strict letter of the law would have been inappropriate because it would not have been the good or the right thing to do.

Rava's approach in this matter is subsequently embraced by the Talmudic sages. Moreover, it can be argued that the Talmud never saw following the strict letter of the law to be sufficient. To prove the point, its sages went so far as to claim that Jerusalem was destroyed because judgments were based strictly on the law and did not go beyond the strict line of justice.[29]

On what basis would the Talmudic sages determine that they could and should go beyond the letter of the law? This is where the exhortation, the meta-command—to "do what is good and right in the eyes of the LORD"—comes into play. The Talmud uses this verse in several well-known instances. For example, the sages in Bava Metzia 24b required individuals to return found objects even if the object was lost in a place where the owner clearly would have given up any hope of its recovery (e.g., if it fell into the sea). In such a case, there is no legal obligation at all. Nonetheless, the sages demanded the return of the lost object! This exemplifies how Jewish law seeks to elevate the individual and to help him or her become better, more moral people.

What should be clear is that, in Jewish law, the legal content of the law is deeply connected to ethics, morality, and justice. Whether a defendant can or cannot be prosecuted for an action may thus be less important than knowing whether it is the "right" thing to do.[30]

In modern times, the interplay between ethics, morality, and the law was frequently discussed by Rabbi Joseph B. Soloveitchik, known reverentially to his students as "the Rav" (the Teacher).[31] One of the Rav's great strengths, both as a religious leader and a philosopher, was his ability to

---

29. The Talmud in Bava Metzia 30b posits the following: "Rebbe Yochanan stated, Jerusalem was destroyed only because they judged according to the law of the Torah. [The students objected] Should then they have judged according to the laws of the sorcerers?! Rather, they insisted narrowly on the strict Torah law, and did not go beyond the letter of the law."

30. This concern for doing the right thing prompted the sages to make an extraordinary claim: "The abrogation of a law is sometimes equivalent to the maintenance of the law," Menachot 99b.

31. The Rav was the undisputed rabbinic leader and leading ideologue of American Modern Orthodoxy for much of the twentieth century. He served as *Rosh Yeshiva* (Dean) of Yeshiva University from 1941 to 1985 and trained scores of American Orthodox rabbis. During this period, he also served as the chief *posek* (legal decisor) of Modern Orthodoxy in America and was one of its chief architects in shaping communal policy.

synthesize Orthodoxy and modernity.[32] Not surprisingly, a topic he often broached was the presumed tension between social norms and theological faith. In noting that for the Greeks and Romans, ethics were secular, the Rav wrote:

> The origin of the term for ethics, *ethos*, is derived from social conventions, social agreements, common habits, common customs, but not the law. Integrating the principle of faith into the system of the moral law was a revolutionary idea. There are in fact no secular ethics.[33]

Thus, for the Rav, neither murder nor theft are inherently wrong or unethical. Humankind has turned away (at least in theory) from both because God commanded "You shall not murder" and "You shall not steal."[34]

More fundamentally, the Rav maintained that a Jew is meant to live a unified life, not one compartmentalized into religious and secular matters or into ethical and legal spheres or, as the Rav put it, into "the street and the synagogue" and "the office and the house of worship."[35]

Law, Justice, and Morality

As we have just seen, the synthesis of ritual and legal matters means that the Talmud must often balance issues of law and morality. This sort of balance is largely absent in the American legal system, as noted by Justice Oliver Wendell Holmes in 1897 in what some consider to be among the most important law review articles ever written.[36] In it, Justice Holmes articulated a path-breaking and widely influential theory of law often referred to as "the bad man" theory. This theory puts forward the following understanding of the purpose of law:

---

32. The Rav studied philosophy and economics at Humboldt University of Berlin (or as it was named until 1949, Friedrich-Wilhelms-Universität). He studied the work of European philosophers and was a life-long student of neo-Kantian thought. He wrote his PhD thesis on the epistemology and metaphysics of the German philosopher Hermann Cohen and graduated with a doctorate in 1932.

33. Lustiger, *Chumash Mesoras Harav*, 434.

34. Exodus 20:19.

35. Lustiger, *Chumash Mesoras Harav*, 435.

36. Jimenez, "Finding the Good in Justice Holmes's Bad Man," 79. Jimenez further opines that Justice Holmes "was perhaps the greatest jurist this country ever produced."

The Purpose of Law

> If you want to know the law and nothing else, you must look at it as a bad man, who cares only for the material consequences which such knowledge enables him to predict, not as a good one, who finds his reasons for conduct, whether inside the law or outside of it, in the vaguer sanctions of conscience.[37]

In other words, says Justice Holmes, the only way to fully appreciate the purpose of the law is to view it from the external perspective of the "bad man" who cares only for the material consequences that such knowledge enables him to predict. This means that the law essentially deals only with people who are not interested in obeying it and who only obey it out of fear of punishment.

In Justice Holmes' understanding of the law, the notions of what is good or right or moral are irrelevant. The law does not exist to set standards or establish parameters in such realms. Instead, the law exists to delineate the consequences of breaking it and is directed at those members of society who ponder how they can avoid punishment. As my colleague and teacher Michael J. Broyde likes to say, such individuals are "law-abiding bad people."

What does Broyde mean by this? These individuals are "good" in the sense that they obey the law, but "bad" in that their only reason for doing so is that the law is deterring them from misconduct.

For Justice Holmes, this is precisely the purpose of the law. The law does not instruct us regarding right and wrong. It simply spells out for us the minimum we must do to avoid punishment.

The Jewish view of the law is very, very different. To see how, let's start with Maimonides, one of the greatest Jewish scholars of all time and the first to write a systematic code of all Jewish law. In his *Guide for the Perplexed*, Maimonides writes at length about the purpose of Jewish law. He first observes that "the general object of the Law is twofold: the well-being of the soul, and the well-being of the body."[38] He continues:

> The well-being of the soul is promoted by correct opinions communicated to the people according to their capacity. Some of these opinions are therefore imparted in a plain form, others allegorically: because certain opinions are in their plain form too strong for the capacity of the common people.

---

37. Holmes, "The Path of the Law," 10.
38. Maimonides, *The Guide for the Perplexed*, Book III, Chapter 27.

> The well-being of the body is established by a proper management of the relations in which we live one to another. This we can attain in two ways: first by removing all violence from our midst: that is to say, that we do not do every one as he pleases, desires, and is able to do; but every one of us does that which contributes towards the common welfare. Secondly, by teaching every one of us such good morals as must produce a good social state. [39]

Maimonides's prescription for obtaining "the well-being of the body"—"a proper management of the relations in which we live one to another"—echoes that which we have previously discussed as the purpose of the law. Yet, he adds a critical differentiating criterion, namely, "good morals."[40]

Another prominent medieval scholar who insisted on the importance of morality in Jewish jurisprudence is Nachmanides.[41] Commenting on the verse "you shall do the right and good," Nachmanides explains that it would be impossible for the verse to enumerate all of the rules necessary and sufficient to govern society.[42] For that reason, after the verse enumerates specific regulations governing interactions between members of society, it commands "you shall do the right and good" as a general principle to guide interactions between individuals in society.[43] Nachmanides in es-

---

39. Maimonides, *The Guide for the Perplexed*, Book III, Chapter 27.

40. Justice Holmes would dismiss such considerations out of hand. For him, the law sets out punishments, reminds people how they are to be punished, and compels obedience through the punishment process. Morals, he would argue, are the purview of rabbis, priests, and imams.

41. Nachmanides was an influential communal leader, biblical exegete, Jewish philosopher, kabbalist, poet, and halakhist. He contributed extensively and profoundly to the whole range of these disciplines. Yet his greatest and most lasting impact was in the realm of halakhic jurisprudence. He penned halakhic treatises in virtually every available genre of halakhic writing—codes, commentaries, compendiums, animadversions, glosses, sermons, exegesis—and he even founded a new genre of halakhic literature known as *hiddushim*. Yet despite his extraordinary contributions to halakhic jurisprudence, contemporary scholarship has remained partial to the other aspects of the Nachmanides's life and works. Scholars have invested substantial resources into studying his kabbalah, his biblical exegesis, his Barcelona Disputation with Pablo Christiani, his role in the Maimonidean Controversy, and his poetry. Few studies have been dedicated to Ramban's halakhic oeuvre, and no study has focused on characterizing Ramban's jurisprudence. Rosensweig, *The Legal Philosophy and Jurisprudence of Rabbi Moshe ben Nahman (Ramban)*.

42. Devarim 6:18.

43. Rosensweig, *The Legal Philosophy and Jurisprudence of Rabbi Moshe ben Nahman*, 331.

sence maintains that morality, that is, questions of what is right and what is wrong, colors almost every aspect of Jewish law.[44]

Judaism's insistence that morality has a role to play in Jewish law is not at odds with Justice Holmes's "bad man" theory. Jewish law frequently informs "good people" to avoid or stay completely away from certain activities. Indeed, much of Jewish law is geared towards telling "good people" the proper thing to do and thereby elevating them.[45] In contrast, American law is largely about constraining "bad people."

Practical Implications

It is interesting to reflect upon the different starting points of Jewish and secular law, but it is more informative to consider concrete instances of how these differences manifest themselves in the day-to-day functioning of these two legal systems. An excellent example is contract law.

There are many different types of contracts in the US legal code, including unilateral contracts,[46] bilateral contracts,[47] simple contracts,[48] and implied contracts.[49] The common element to all contracts is that they are legally binding agreements between parties to create mutual obligations that businesses and individuals use to protect their interests. Contracts outline

---

44. We will further explore the ramifications of this approach later in this chapter.

45. These laws, as embodied in the Torah's positive commandments, are voluntary. There is no mechanism in Judaism for coercing positive commandments. Yet as *Tosafot*, a major decisor in Jewish law, points out, Jewish law is also replete with negative commandments, and, definitionally, almost all negative commandments are "bad man rules" that can be enforced by the court system. That is the nature of negative commandments: the legal system enforces them. This is one area n which one could argue that Jewish law and Holmes's "bad man" theory come together.

46. A unilateral contract is a one-sided contract agreement in which an offeror promises to pay only after the completion of a task by the offeree. In this type of agreement, the offeror is the only party with a contractual obligation.

47. A bilateral contract is a contract in which both parties exchange promises to perform. One party's promise serves as consideration for the promise of the other. As a result, each party is an obligor on that party's own promise and an obligee on the other's promise.

48. A simple contract is a contract made orally or in writing or both rather than a contract made under seal. Simple contracts require consideration to be valid, but simple contracts may be implied from the conduct of parties bound by the contract.

49. An implied-in-law contract is the restitution recovery at law, which imposes a legal obligation to an unjustly enriched party to compensate the other party. It is not applied only when there is no contract but also when there is a total breach of contract.

the specific terms of engagement for a transaction. They can also dictate legal consequences if a party tries to break the agreement.

The three essential components of any contract are the offer, the acceptance, and the consideration. If all three of these characteristics are not present, a document is not considered a contract. When two individuals enter into a binding contract, should one party fail to fulfill the conditions set forth in the contract, the second party can sue for damages. Even in the absence of actual damages, the second party can sue for lost profits.[50]

Consider this example.

Party A agrees to sell Party B fifty widgets at a cost of $1.00 each, with a delivery scheduled within thirty days. Party B agrees to pay $50 for the widgets, but only upon delivery. In the interim, Party B arranges to sell the widgets to the local hardware store for $3.00 each, thus netting $100 in profit upon completion of the transaction. Unfortunately, on day twenty, Party A declares that they cannot or will not fulfill the contract. Party B has suffered no damages because payment was only required upon delivery of the widgets, but Party B has lost out on $100 in profit and can sue Party A to recover these lost profits.

The reason for Party A's failure to fulfill the contract is not relevant in American law. Perhaps it was due to ill-will (the two parties got into a fight and are no longer speaking) or even unforeseen circumstances (Party A's widget factory was struck by lightning and burned to the ground). American law treats contracts as purely economic agreements. There is no morality undergirding them.

Let's turn now to Jewish contract law, which was developed at a time when other ancient systems of law (such as Babylonian and Assyrian law) allowed creditors to secure repayment of a debt by enslaving debtors or the members of their family. Early Roman law went even farther. It granted creditors the right, after certain preliminary procedures, to put defaulting debtors to death and take their proportionate share of the body if there were several creditors.[51]

---

50. Every United States jurisdiction has adopted the rule that one may sue for and collect lost profits if said loss was proven with reasonable certainty. Despite this universal adoption of the language, courts have never really explained what they mean by the term "reasonable certainty." Lloyd, "The Reasonable Certainty Requirement In Lost Profits Litigation."

51. "Law of Obligations."

The Purpose of Law

All this was an anathema to the Talmudic sages. Jewish law does not recognize any form of enslavement of a debtor.[52] Moreover, the sages strongly encouraged creditors to act mercifully toward borrowers and not, for example, to take the latter's basic essentials as collateral or enter their homes for the purpose of seizing a pledge.[53]

None of this addresses what could, and sometimes does, occur on occasion. People make commitments they cannot fulfill. So what is to be done in such circumstances?

American contract law has a simple answer: give them money. Failure to fulfill valid contracts has financial consequences. Jewish law, however, recognizes that not every commitment, contractual or otherwise, can be monetized. Take our widget example from above. There was certainly a commitment by Party A to deliver the widgets, but there was no transaction at all. Party B neither pre-paid nor gave a deposit on the order. Without a transaction, there is no binding commitment. At best, it is merely a promise regarding a future action, and, as such, it cannot be monetized.

Does this mean that Party B has no recourse? The Talmud does not think so.[54]

Time and time again, the Talmud rules that individuals such as Party A are "liable under the laws of Heaven," and they are often described as "wicked," having "behaved with deceit," having "acted in the manner of Sodom," "lacking in honesty," and having engaged in a behavior "that is not pleasing to the spirit of the sages." We even find a case in the Talmud in which the offended party is not only given the right to publicly curse the one who wronged him, the curse that one is permitted to use is even spelled out: "The One who punished the generation of the flood, the generation of the dispersion, the people of Sodom and Gomorrah, and the Egyptians who drowned in the sea, should punish the person who does not stand by his word."[55]

Here, then, is a crucial difference between Jewish contract law and secular law. By strongly condemning these actions, the Talmudic sages

---

52. The Torah does refer to and permit two instances of bondsmanship. The first involves a thief who lacks the means to make restitution (Exodus 22:2); the second deals with individuals who voluntarily sells themselves on account of utter poverty (Leviticus 25:39).

53. See Exodus 22:24–26 and Deuteronomy 24:6, 10–13.

54. The examples that follow are taken from Friedman, "Talmudic Ethics and its Reliance on Values Rather than Rules," 10–11.

55. Talmud Bavli Baba Metzia 48a.

make clear that in such matters, it does not matter whether or not one is technically breaking the law. Wrong is wrong. Unethical is unethical, even in cases in which a defendant cannot be prosecuted for an action. In American law, unmonetizable breaches of integrity are essentially without consequences.[56]

One final case will prove this point.

The Talmud discusses a case in which two parties have concluded negotiations leading to a sale and are in the process of closing that deal. Unexpectedly, a third party jumps in and makes the purchase. The interloper cannot be prosecuted legally, but is described as a "wicked person."[57] By characterizing the act as the mark of a wicked person, the sages seek to establish a deterrent to its perpetrator as well as to the seller, who may be dissuaded from becoming party to a wicked act.[58]

By focusing on what is right and not solely on what is legal, Jewish law seeks to elevate and refine the individual. Conversely, emphasizing that which is legal (so as to avoid that which is illegal) above all else is a core element to the constraints secular law imposes on people.

---

56. It is worthwhile noting that in debating one's obligation to repay a debt, R. Papa maintains that is it no more than a religious duty, meaning, it is a *mitzvah* for a person to fulfill his promise, not a legal obligation. (Talmud Bavli Ketuvot 86a) R. Huna, however, expressed the opinion—which was shared by the majority of the scholars and according to which the *halakha* was decided—that the duty of repaying a debt was also a legal obligation. Not merely a legal obligation, but also a legal obligation. The religious duty to do so remains in place.

57. Talmud Bavli Kiddushin 59a.

58. Friedman, "Talmudic Ethics and its Reliance on Values Rather than Rules," 11.

CHAPTER THREE

Different Notions of Foundational Texts

AT THEIR CORE, ALL legal systems have the same purpose of regulating and harmonizing the human activity within their respective societies,[1] but (and please forgive the bad pun), not all legal systems are created equal. This is particularly true for the two best-known types of legal systems: those that are common law-based and those that are civil law-based.[2]

Common law is primarily derived from custom and judicial precedent rather than statutes. It is most often associated with England, where it originated, but is also in force in approximately eighty countries formerly part of or influenced by the former British Empire. In this system, settlements of disputes were conducted on a purely local level, which meant that each region acted independently and without the knowledge of what other localities were doing. In other words, common law systems are not built upon broadly based foundational documents. Rather, the rights and obligations of individuals flow from the nature of their personal status within the system.[3]

And what is civil law? The term "civil law" is derived from the Latin words "*jus civile*," a reference to laws in ancient Rome that were designed to

---

1. Dainow, "The Civil Law and the Common Law: Some Points of Comparison," 419.

2. A focus on these two legal systems makes sense for the purposes of this book. Yet, as Dainow notes, it does not negate the significance of the different legal systems of the Asiatic countries or those of the Scandinavian countries.

3. Dainow, "The Civil Law and the Common Law: Some Points of Comparison," 422.

apply solely to its citizens. Today's civil law systems are largely grounded in the Roman legal tradition as set forth in *Corpus Juris Civilus*, (Body of Civil Law), a collection of laws and legal interpretations compiled under the East Roman (Byzantine) Emperor Justinian I between 528 and 565 CE.[4] Civil law is the most widespread legal system in the world and is used in various forms in approximately 150 countries. Simply put, its laws are organized into systematic written codes, and the authoritative sources for such codes are principally legislation, especially codifications in constitutions or statutes enacted by governments. These are, of course, the very definition of foundational documents and, as such, they establish the basis for and determine the nature of the legal system.[5]

The American legal system remains firmly within the common law tradition brought to the North American colonies from England. Yet, traces of the civil law tradition and its importance in the hemisphere may be found within state legal traditions across the United States.[6]

THE LIMITS OF FOUNDATIONAL TEXTS

Students of history are surely familiar with the notion of foundational documents such as the Code of Hammurabi[7] and the Magna Carta.[8] More advanced students might have even studied lesser-known (but

---

4. "Field listing - Legal system."

5. Dainow, "The Civil Law and the Common Law: Some Points of Comparison," 421.

6. The most prominent example is Louisiana, where state law is based on civil law as a result of Louisiana's history as a French and Spanish territory prior to its purchase from France in 1803. "The Common Law and Civil Law Traditions."

7. The Code of Hammurabi is a legal text composed during 1755–1750 BCE, purportedly by Hammurabi, sixth king of the First Dynasty of Babylon. A collection of 282 rules, it established standards for commercial interactions and set fines and punishments to meet the requirements of justice in ancient Babylonia. It is the longest, best-organized, and best-preserved legal text from the ancient Near East.

8. Magna Carta was issued in June 1215 and was the first document to put into writing the principle that the king and his government was not above the law. It sought to prevent the king from exploiting his power, and placed limits of royal authority by establishing law as a power in itself.

Different Notions of Foundational Texts

historically significant) texts such as the Ninety-five Theses[9] and the Mayflower Compact.[10]

In America, even those unversed in history are aware of the country's foundational documents: the Declaration of Independence, the Constitution, the Bill of Rights, and even the Federalist Papers.[11] People often assume that these are the pillars of America's legal system, both in philosophical and practical terms. This is a flawed assumption. These documents are indeed foundational from a philosophical perspective, but not from a legal perspective. Why is that? In brief, for a text to be foundational for our purposes, it must serve in some capacity as a basis for the underlying legal system. Yet it need not be binding. A good example is the Declaration of Independence.

Most school children in America knowsome of its words by heart: "We hold these truths to be self-evident, that all men are created equal, that they are endowed by their Creator with certain unalienable Rights, that among these are Life, Liberty and the pursuit of Happiness."[12] These

9. The Ninety-five Theses is a list of propositions for an academic disputation written in 1517 by Martin Luther, then a professor of moral theology at the University of Wittenberg, Germany. The Theses is considered to have launched the Protestant Reformation and Protestantism.

10. The Mayflower Compact was the first governing document of Plymouth Colony. It was written by the men aboard the *Mayflower* and signed aboard ship on November 21, 1620. At a commemoration ceremony for the 300th anniversary of the *Mayflower* landing, then Massachusetts governor Calvin Coolidge, who became the thirtieth US President a few years later, said the following about the Mayflower Compact: "The compact which they signed was an event of the greatest importance. It was the foundation of liberty based on law and order, and that tradition has been steadily upheld. They drew up a form of government which has been designated as the first real constitution of modern times. It was democratic, an acknowledgment of liberty under law and order and the giving to each person the right to participate in the government, while they promised to be obedient to the laws." "Mayflower Compact."

11. In modern times, constitutions are almost always embodied in a written document. However, the simple idea that a nation's constitution should be written down is an American innovation. Lee, "Civil Law's Influence on American Constitutionalism."

12. Social studies curricula across the nation include knowledge of the Declaration of Independence as early as fourth grade. This means that, with help, students are expected to be able to "read and analyze the text of the Declaration of Independence to determine important principles that it contains including inalienable rights, government by the consent of the governed and the redress of grievances" according to the social studies standards of certain states. (In California, the state standards say students in grade 1 should be able to identify the Declaration of Independence, and know the people and events associated with [it].) The topic is also covered repeatedly in a variety of ways in sixth through twelfth grade. For instance, students in grades six through eight should

words have shaped American thinking in many areas, and the notion of what constitutes an "unalienable right" is often debated in our times.[13] The lofty principles articulated in this document may well have resonated with the drafters of the US Constitution and most certainly did with those who wrote the Bill of Rights. Nonetheless, everyone involved in America's legal system, from judge to jurist, understands that the Declaration of Independence is not a legally binding text.

This does not diminish its importance. Indeed, every legal system has important documents like it, texts that are foundational to the history of a nation and that serve as touchstones in defining the nation's goals and aspirations. Nations—and the legal systems that sustain them—cannot exist without such foundational texts. They must exist, but they need not be legally binding.

There is another type of legally binding text that, while foundational, is of little practical use. This is because they are so broad and so vague that they offer little real guidance in difficult cases. The Jewish tradition wrestles precisely with such a text.

The Torah is unquestionably Judaism's foundational text. Every observant Jew sees it as binding. Yet when it tells us not to kill or murder, what are we to do with this command? It may set forth an important moral "redline," but it leaves unanswered questions such as, may I kill in self-defense? May I kill in times of war? This underscores for us a very basic premise. For a legal text to be valuable and worthwhile as a foundational document, it must provide enough discussion and complexity to actually help guide people in matters that might be in dispute. Being foundational in the literal sense (as the Torah certainly is) is not the same as being foundational in a legal sense (which, in certain instances, it is not).

---

be able to "analyze the Declaration of Independence to determine the historical context and political philosophies that influenced its creation." Students in grades nine through twelve are expected to "apply the concepts of natural law, social contract, due process of law, and popular sovereignty to explain the purposes and legacy of the Declaration of Independence." Czopek, "US public schools are still teaching about the Declaration of Independence."

13. Are reproductive rights an "unalienable right?" Are LBGTQ rights an "unalienable?" And so on. See, for example, "Natural Law, Human Rights, and Unalienable Rights."

Different Notions of Foundational Texts

FOUNDATIONAL TEXTS IN AMERICAN LAW

Without a doubt, the Constitution is the great foundational legal text of the United States. It is a nuanced legal document written by people who intended it to be binding. When one delves into the Constitution, there is a clear sense that America's founders had a vision for how the system would function, in part because it was crafted with care to address hard issues of law. It is both foundational and nuanced enough to make it worthwhile to look at when confronting hard cases.

For all its strengths, the flaws of the Constitution became apparent during the ratification process.[14] It lacked any definition of individual rights, the very same rights that the colonists charged King George with trampling upon in the Declaration of Independence. The Bill of Rights—the first Ten Amendments to the Constitution—were therefore added to the Constitution to address this.

The significance of the Bill of Rights goes beyond the protections it affords Americans. It also demonstrates explicitly and directly that this foundational binding text of the American legal system is not closed. It can be amended and changed, adapted and revised.[15] And, because of this, it has to be interpreted continuously, in a cyclical way. This is achieved by examining whether any of the Amendments have changed the text itself, and this quite literally makes the Constitution a living text.

What happens when a practical legal problem arises that cannot be solved with the text of the Constitution? We amend the text, and because the Constitution is a living document and because there are well-established procedures for amending the text, we are comfortable doing so, even if we do so rather infrequently.[16]

---

14. The process of ratification of the Constitution involved each of the thirteen original states convening conventions in which representatives voted for or against ratification. Article VII of the Constitution states, "The Ratification of the Conventions of nine States, shall be sufficient for the Establishment of this Constitution between the States so ratifying the Same."

15. An amendment may be proposed by a two-thirds vote of both Houses of Congress, or, if two-thirds of the States request one, by a convention called for that purpose. The amendment must then be ratified by three-fourths of the State legislatures, or three-fourths of conventions called in each State for ratification.

16. More than 11,000 amendments to the Constitution of the United States have been proposed, but only twenty-seven have been ratified, including the ten that make up the Bill of Rights. The Constitution was last amended in 1992. "Amendments to the Constitution."

Between the Laws of God and Man

The fact that the Constitution can be amended in no way negates the importance of precedent in the American legal system. Precedent refers to a court decision that is considered as authority for deciding subsequent cases involving identical or similar facts or similar legal issues.[17] It requires courts to apply the law in the same manner to cases with the same facts. In short, precedent ensures that individuals in similar situations are treated alike instead of based on a particular judge's personal views.[18]

In the book of Ecclesiastes, it states that "there is nothing new under the sun."[19] This is certainly the case with concerns about the Supreme Court turning away from the "sanctity" of precedent. It may feel to some that these are newly held concerns, as the Court has taken a sharp conservative turn in recent years. A quick look back to the early 1990s demonstrates that this is not so.

At that time, national attention was focused on the extent to which the Supreme Court Justices were following precedents with whose reasoning or holdings they disagreed. Concerns grew even greater when Justice Thurgood Marshall abruptly resigned from the Court on the last day of its 1990—1991 term, an action seemingly fueled by his frustrations over the Court's overruling of two criminal procedure precedents on that same day in *Payne v. Tennessee*[20] and over the possibility that "scores of established constitutional liberties are now ripe for reconsideration."[21] In the aftermath of Justice Marshall's resignation, including Justice Clarence Thomas's contentious confirmation proceedings, many Senators and concerned Americans

---

17. Precedent is incorporated into the doctrine of *stare decisis*, which is a Latin term that means "let the decision stand" or "to stand by things decided." *Stare decisis* is a foundational concept in the American legal system. To put it simply, *stare decisis* holds that courts and judges should honor "precedent"—or the decisions, rulings, and opinions from prior cases. Respect for precedents gives the law consistency and makes interpretations of the law more predictable—and less seemingly random. "Understanding Stare Decisis."

18. It should be obvious that a case cannot be used as precedent in instances in which the facts or issues of a case differ from those in previous cases. Indeed, the Supreme Court in 2004 in *Cooper Industries, Inc. v. Aviall Services, Inc.* reiterated that "[q]uestions which merely lurk on the record, neither brought to the attention of the court nor ruled upon, are not to be considered as . . . precedent." Therefore, a prior decision serves as precedent only for issues, given the particular facts, that the court explicitly considered in reaching its decision. *Cooper Industries, Inc. v. Aviall Services, Inc.*, 543 U.S. 157 (2004).

19. Ecclesiastes 1:9.

20. *Payne v. Tennessee*, 501 U.S. 808 (1991).

21. Gerhardt, "The Role of Precedent in Constitutional Decisionmaking and Theory," 70.

Different Notions of Foundational Texts

expressed their frustration over the prospect of the Court's dismantlement of a significant number of precedents recognizing protection of individual liberties in such varied areas of constitutional law as abortion, affirmative action, separation of church and state, and criminal procedure.[22]

Nevertheless, since 2005, when John G. Roberts, Jr. was confirmed as Chief Justice, the tone and tenor of the Supreme Court has changed. Under Roberts' stewardship, originalism, that is, interpreting the Constitution as it would have been understood or was intended to be understood at the time it was written, has become an increasingly important underpinning for the Court's decisions. For the conservative Justices on the Court, this was a necessary remedy for what they believed was ill-advised judicial activism evident in some of the Court's prior rulings. This, in turn, made Roberts' Court more willing and ready to overturn established precedents. A notable example is the Court's holding in *District of Columbia v. Heller*.[23] That case focused on a District of Columbia law that banned handgun possession. Specifically, the law made it a crime to carry an unregistered firearm. In the case, what was at issue was that a policeman, who had applied to register a handgun he wished to keep at home, was denied his request. The officer then filed a suit seeking, on Second Amendment grounds, to enjoin the city from enforcing the ban on handgun registration.

The text of the Second Amendment is familiar to many: "A well regulated Militia, being necessary to the security of a free State, the right of the people to keep and bear Arms, shall not be infringed." Until *Heller*, this amendment was understood for decades by the courts as simply guaranteeing the right of states to form militias. As early as 1875, in *United States v. Cruikshank*, the Court ruled that "[t]he right to bear arms is not granted by the Constitution; neither is it in any manner dependent upon that instrument for its existence. The Second Amendment means no more than that it shall not be infringed upon by Congress, and has no other effect than to restrict the powers of the National Government."[24] In 1939, in *United States v. Miller*, the Court reached a similar conclusion: "the Second Amendment does not guarantee an individual the right to keep and bear a sawed-off double-barrel shotgun. . . . [and] because possessing a sawed-off double barrel shotgun does not have a reasonable relationship to the preservation

---

22. Gerhardt, "The Role of Precedent in Constitutional Decisionmaking and Theory," 70.

23. *District of Columbia v. Heller*, 554 U.S. 570 (2008).

24. *United States v. Cruikshank*, 92 U.S. 542 (1875).

or efficiency of a well-regulated militia, the Second Amendment does not protect the possession of such an instrument."[25]

Even Robert Bork, one of the early architects of originalism, itself an invention of the 1970s, strenuously argued in 1989 that the original intention of the Second Amendment was "to guarantee the right of states to form militia, not for individuals to bear arms."[26]

None of this deterred the conservatives on the Court in their *Heller* ruling. Writing for the majority, Justice Antonin Scalia began his analysis by noting "[i]n interpreting this text, we are guided by the principle that '[t]he Constitution was written to be understood by the voters; its words and phrases were used in their normal and ordinary as distinguished from technical meaning." He went on to argue that "the Second Amendment is naturally divided into two parts" and then proceeded to "decouple[e] the right to bear arms for the establishment of 'a well regulated Militia." This provided the rationale for overturning years of precedent and allowed the Court to rule that the Second Amendment gives individuals a self-standing, constitutionally protected right to gun ownership.

The confirmation of Justice Amy Coney Barrett in late October 2020 raised to four the number of Justices who self-identify as full-blown originalists (Thomas, Gorsuch, Kavanaugh, and Barrett). A fifth, Justice Alito is an on and off again originalist.[27] There was thus little surprise when these Justices took the lead in *Dobbs v. Jackson*[28] and overturned another long-standing precedent, a woman's right to an abortion that had been ruled (by a 7 to 2 majority) to be a constitutionally protected right by the Court in 1972 in *Roe v. Wade*.[29]

Justice Alito wrote the majority opinion, joined by Justices Thomas, Gorsuch, Kavanaugh, and Barrett. His opinion stated that the critical

---

25. *United States v. Miller*, 307 U.S. 174 (1939).
26. Lepore, "The Supreme Court's Selective Memory."
27. Segal, "An Originalism Scorecard Since Justice Barrett Arrived on the Court."
28. *Dobbs v. Jackson Women's Health Organization*, 597 U.S. 215 (2022).
29. The Court expressly ruled that "The Due Process Clause of the Fourteenth Amendment protects against state action the right to privacy, and a woman's right to choose to have an abortion falls within that right to privacy. A state law that broadly prohibits abortion without respect to the stage of pregnancy or other interests violates that right. Although the state has legitimate interests in protecting the health of pregnant women and the 'potentiality of human life,' the relative weight of each of these interests varies over the course of pregnancy, and the law must account for this variability." *Roe v. Wade*, 410 U.S. 113 (1973).

question in Dobbs was whether the Constitution "properly understood" confers a right to obtain an abortion. In answering this question in the negative, the Court observed that the Constitution makes no express references to abortion, nor argued the Court, was abortion deeply rooted in the nation's history and traditions. The Court also noted that the history of abortion in the US is "as a crime," and it went on to highlight that, when the Fourteenth Amendment was adopted, three-quarters of the States had made abortion a crime at any stage of pregnancy. The Court explained that this was true until *Roe*, which had ruled that the right to abortion was protected by the Fourteenth Amendment's guarantee of liberty. Thus, based on their originalist read of the Fourteenth Amendment in *Dobbs*, "liberty" would not recognize abortion as a fundamental right rooted in the nature, history, or traditions of the nation. The Court even concluded that "*Roe* either ignored or misstated this history."[30]

Critics of the *Dobbs* decision angrily pointed out that the very Justices who voted to overturn *Roe* had publicly stated that in their confirmation hearings before the US Senate that *Roe* was "precedent" or "established law."[31]

If the overturning of precedent is driven by partisan politics, as some now claim, perhaps there is cause for real concern. However, it is possible, as one legal scholar has suggested, that "the Court's review of its precedents [are] a dialogue in which the Justices each consider the 'substantially countervailing considerations' for no longer preserving the values their predecessors previously have endorsed for controlling the operation of government."[32] This same scholar goes on to conclude that "this kind of

30. Dobbs v. Jackson Women's Health Organization, 597 U.S. 215 (2022). Let me note with comment that the Court argued that linking abortion to a right to autonomy or to "define one's concept of existence" would also license fundamental rights to "illicit drug use, [or] prostitution."

31. During questioning, Justice Brett Kavanaugh avoided answering whether Roe v. Wade was correctly decided, or how he might rule in a future case challenging that court ruling. Instead, Kavanaugh repeatedly said that Roe v. Wade was "settled as precedent." Justice Neil Gorsuch said that the Roe decision was "precedent," but declined to call it "super precedent," a loosely defined term indicating a deeply rooted, repeatedly upheld precedent. He also declined to give his opinion on whether he thought the court's ruling was correct. Justice Amy Coney Barrett, was upfront about her history of supporting the Catholic Church's teaching on "the sacredness of life from conception to natural death." And she was noncommittal during Senate confirmation hearings in October 2020 about whether she might overturn Roe v. Wade. Gore, Farley, and Robertson, "What Gorsuch, Kavanaugh and Barrett Said About Roe at Confirmation Hearings."

32. Gerhardt, "The Role of Precedent in Constitutional Decisionmaking and

decision making is necessary to protect the rule of law, and the institutions and expectations built around it, and to allow some flexibility and deviation from the past when there are substantial or important reasons to do so."[33]

If this is the case, and I leave it to those more versed in the law than I am to decide, it would make preserving or revising precedent a living process in the same way that amending the Constitution makes it a living document.

FOUNDATIONAL TEXTS IN JEWISH LAW[34]

Jewish and American law vary in two important ways when it comes to when and why a text is seen as foundational. The first involves how each determines that a foundational document has become binding.

The most important of America's foundational documents, the Constitution, is, as we have seen, binding, but not closed. The converse is true of Judaism's most famous foundational document, the Torah. It is closed. Maimonides said as much in his commentary to the Mishnah: "Nothing can be added to or subtracted from either the written Torah or the oral Torah. It is thus written (Deuteronomy 13:1), 'You shall not add to it, nor subtract from it.'"[35] That being said, the Torah may be closed, but it is not binding, as we have discussed. The Torah is the moral foundation of Judaism, but it cannot serve as its legal foundation, because its words frequently lack the depth and complexity needed to resolve difficult legal issues.

Where, then, do we find a text that meets the definition of a foundational legal document for Judaism, something that looks much more like a constitution or a code book? That would be the Mishnah, a written compilation of oral traditions compiled and redacted by Rabbi Yehudah Ha-Nasi sometime around the year 200 CE. It is a systemic and complete legal framework designed to cover all areas of Jewish law. Moreover, the Mishnah has sections, codes, and chapters, like a constitution, and it is organized in a fairly logical way. Thus, were one to look for, say, the laws of divorce, they are easy to find. In total, there are six orders of the Mishnah, and one

---

Theory," 75.

33. Gerhardt, "The Role of Precedent in Constitutional Decisionmaking and Theory," 75.

34. Special thanks is due to Rabbi Michael J. Broyde for his assistance with this section.

35. Talmud Bavli Sanhedrin, chapter 10.

Different Notions of Foundational Texts

of them is devoted to family law.³⁶ The Mishnah's family law section, which has twelve chapters, is where one would find details about divorce. Other topics are similarly easy to find.³⁷

This level of organization and ease of use stands in stark contrast to the Torah. In the Torah, nothing is well-organized. Indeed, we are not always sure why laws appear where they do in the text nor do we always grasp the Torah's seemingly haphazard and disorganized structure. Yet, for all its organization, the Mishnah remains a problematic text because it frequently and simultaneously records multiple opinions on the same issue. This means that the Mishnah lacks the central characteristic of a law code: instead of a single definitive opinion, it gives us more than one opinion. Still, it is not haphazard in its methodology. It follows basic rules for the opinions it cites. For instance, it typically labels minority and majority opinions as such. When it brings multiple opinions on a topic, it states quite clearly that "this is the opinion of the Rabbis" and "this is Rabbi So-and-So's opinion."

Next in Judaism's chain of foundational legal texts is the Talmud. Some would even argue that the Talmud is Judaism's key foundational legal document. Like the Torah, it is a closed document, and while it is intensely studied by students of Jewish law, it is hard to describe it as binding. Why? Because it is a very diverse complex document, and boiling it down to a single reasonable opinion cannot be done on most matters that are in dispute. A person can study the Talmud daily and still realize, upon finishing a particular Talmudic text, that the normative Jewish law for the topic at hand is still undecided. Or the Talmud will discuss the same topic in three different places and reach different conclusions in each place.

None of this detracts from the Talmud's standing as one of the foundational texts of Jewish law. The importance of the Talmud is that it formulates a broad range of opinions that all post-Talmudic legal opinions must acknowledge. Moreover, these later opinions must also be consistent with these Talmudic rulings. The challenge is, how to deal with the Talmud's many and oft-time conflicting opinions?

Two distinct schools of thought arose to address this conundrum.

---

36. The Mishnah consists of six major sections, or orders (*sedarim*) that contain 63 tractates (*massekhtaot*) in all, each of which is further divided into chapters: *Zera' im* ("Seeds"); *Mo' ed* ("Festival"); *Nashim* ("Women"); *Neziqin* ("Damages"); *Qodashim* ("Holy Things"); and *Ṭohorot* ("Purifications").

37. Topics not found in the Mishnah are lacking because Rabbi Yehuda HaNasi did not understand them to be the law.

The first, led by the Rif (Rabbi Yitzhak Alfasi[38]) and Maimonides, argues for figuratively editing out every superfluous or incorrect opinions in the Talmud. The goal was to produce a simpler and more coherent Jewish law, and to this end, both scholars authored codes of Jewish law. The Rif's codification, *Sefer ha-Halakhot* ("Book of Laws"), is one of the greatest and most important works in the halachic system, one that left its mark on the study and determination of Jewish law in every subsequent generation.[39] Maimonides codification, *Mishneh Torah* (literally, "Repetition of the Torah"), ranks among the greatest and most innovative Jewish legal texts of all time. Its significance stems from its systematic categorizations and clear explanations of all aspects of Jewish observance, including those applicable only in Temple times.

The second approach was championed by Rashi[40] and *Tosafot*[41] and all of the medievalists who followed them. They wrote commentaries on the Talmud, elaborating on it and explaining the various opinions, each in its own place. Sometimes their commentaries reached normative conclusions of Jewish law. Other times they expanded the range of options available to students of Jewish law through their analytic reasoning. As compared to Maimonides, *Tosafot* were not attempting to simplify the Talmud. Instead, they were endeavoring to make it more complex.

Others followed the lead of *Tosafot*, and from around 1200 to about 1450, numerous robust commentaries on the Talmud were written that expounded upon and expanded its theoretical legal constructs. The common element to these commentaries? They rejected Maimonides's pattern of simplification, notwithstanding his status as the greatest Jewish law sage of the last two thousand years! It is only in the 1500s, when Rabbi Josef Karo[42]

38. The Rif, who lived from 1013 to 1103, was the greatest Talmudic scholar of his era.

39. Elon, "Rabbi Isaac Alfasi."

40. Rabbi Solomon ben Isaac, known as Rashi (based on an acronym of the Hebrew initials of his name), is one of the most influential Jewish commentators in history.

41. *Tosafot* is a term used to describe a commentary that appears in current editions of the Talmud that was written primarily by a group of scholars in France and Germany in the twelfth and thirteenth centuries. Many of these scholars were members of Rashi's family.

42. Rabbi Yosef Caro (1488–1575) was an outstanding lawyer and mystic. He wrote a commentary, entitled *Kesef Mishnah* to Maimonides's code and another commentary, his greatest work, on the *Tur* of Jacob ben Asher, to which he gave the title *Bet Yosef* (House of Joseph), because in it he provided a home for all of the legal opinions held by the jurists of the past. The *Bet Yosef* is probably the keenest work of legal analysis in the history of Jewish law. Jacobs, "Joseph Caro."

Different Notions of Foundational Texts

began his *Shulchan Aruch*, that we see a move to return to Maimonides's basic mission, which was to simplify Jewish law into straightforward rules that can readily be understood. Rabbi Karo was so committed to simplicity that he essentially deleted those elements of Maimonides's code not needed in modern times (such as the laws of sacrifices or the laws of kings). He then adds things that Maimonides left out and corrects Maimonides few "errors." The result? An even more simplified code of Jewish law.

At last, it would seem, Judaism had a foundational, binding legal text. A reasonable, perhaps aspirational assumption, but, in the end, an incorrect one. The trend begun by *Tosafot*, that is, a preference for an expanded range of legal options, resurfaced and pushed back against Rabbi Karo's attempts to craft a simplified code of Jewish law. Within 100 years of the dissemination of the *Shulchan Aruch*, seven super-commentaries were written on it and with them, the model of complexity reappeared.[43] By 1895, the standard Vilna edition of the *Shulchan Aruch* contained more than 100 commentaries, yielding an ill-determined Jewish law code that left Jewish law without its sought-after foundational text.

All this highlights a second critical difference between Jewish and American law in terms of foundational texts. In America, there is consensus about which texts are binding, and that consensus exists in all states and in all jurisdictions. This is not true in Judaism, and understanding why requires a bit of historical background.

Two distinct communities (in the most general sense of the word) of Jews developed during their century-long diaspora following the destruction of the Second Temple: Ashkenazim and Sephardim. The difference between Ashkenazi and Sephardi Jews is primarily based on their historical origins. *Ashkenaz* is the Hebrew word for Germany, and the term Ashkenazi Jews initially referred to Jews residing in Germany, where Ashkenazi Jewry began.[44] However, most European Jews ultimately came to be known

---

43. In our editions of the *Shulchan Aruch*, there are several primary commentators on Rabbi Caro's basic text. By section of the *Shulchan Aruch*, they are: on *Orach Chayim*, Magen Avraham and Taz; on *Yoreh De'ah*, Shakh and Taz; on *Even Ha'ezer*, Beit Shmuel and Chelkat Mechokek; and on *Choshen Mishpat*, Shakh and Me'irat Einayim.

44. From a historical perspective, northern Europe was settled fairly recently by Jews. A small number of Jews are believed to have settled in western Germany and northern France in the ninth to tenth centuries, especially along the Rhine River. Their population grew, and they generally migrated towards the east, especially to Poland. By the twelfth century, Jewish communities were established as far as Russia. Later, in the eighteenth century and after, Jews migrated back westward (as well as to America) in response to the much harsher conditions in eastern Europe. Rosenfeld, "Ashkenazi vs Sephardic Jews."

as "Ashkenazi" Jews, regardless of their country of residence. Today about 80 percent of world Jewry are Ashkenazi.[45]

Sephardic Jews literally mean Spanish Jews as *Sepharad* means Spain in Hebrew.[46] Jews lived there, as well as in North Africa, the Middle East, and parts of southeast Europe since antiquity. Spain was an especially prosperous and tolerant land from the eighth century under Muslim rule, and Jewish communities flourished there, both economically and religiously, until their expulsion in 1492.[47] These were the original Sephardi Jews. This term, however, is not so precise today, as it is loosely applied (especially by non-Sephardim) to all non-Ashkenazi Jews.

The cultural differences between Ashkenazi and Sephardi Jews can be significant, ranging from the foods they eat to various religious rituals in the home and synagogue. These differences are particularly pronounced in terms of how each group views foundational texts in Jewish law, a question driven by the Talmud's diverse and non-binding opinions.

The Sephardim have a simple solution to this dilemma. They embraced the concept of having one individual rabbi, one with worldwide credentials such as Rabbi Karo, establish a foundational text once and for all, based on the teachings of Maimonides. For Sephardim, this means that the text of the *Shulchan Aruch* is binding, and everyone must follow the legal opinions it codifies. This is particularly true among the Sephardi communities in Israel, thanks to the efforts of the former Sephardi Chief Rabbi Ovadia Yosef and his son Rabbi Yitzhak (who currently occupies the position of Sephardic Chief Rabbi in Israel). In fact, Rav Ovadia and his son have been on a sixty-year campaign to eliminate from the Sephardi community all "deviant" versions of Jewish law, that is those which are inconsistent with the text of the *Shulchan Aruch*. This reflects their position that contemporary Jewish law does indeed have a foundational text and that text is the *Shulchan Aruch*.

---

45. The percentage was much higher before the Holocaust.

46. The term *Sepharad* also appears in the Bible (Obadiah 1:20) although the original meaning is disputed.

47. When Jews were expelled (or forced to convert) from Spain in 1492 and from neighboring Portugal in 1497, they fled to many existing areas of Jewish habitation, especially North Africa and the Ottoman Empire. Many of these lands thus became much more closely aligned with Sephardic traditions, despite vast differences in custom and culture between the existing Jewish communities and the newly arriving Spanish and Portuguese Jews.

Different Notions of Foundational Texts

The Ashkenazim disagree. While many Ashkenazim rely on Rama's (Rabbi Moshe Isserles) glosses of the *Shulchan Aruch* and the legal opinions poses, they do not view this as a foundational text.[48] In fact, Ashkenazim essentially deny that there *is* a single foundational text of Jewish law. Instead, they perceive Jewish law as a corpus—a compendium of opinions—that is continuously open for authorities of Jewish law to make decisions based on what best fits the needs of the times. As such, the Ashkenazi tradition of Jewish law much more intensely resembles British common law, meaning, it looks like codified statutory law.

Many argue that the Ashkenazi approach to the law is too complex, and there is some truth to this. A standard code of Jewish law with twenty significant commentaries is not particularly helpful in solving real life disputes. In fact, it signals a quasi-return to the Talmudic model, where the parameters of the legal debates produce the limits of what can be done, and those deciding the law must choose between the opposite ends of the spectrum. On occasion, some topics even remain off limits because they are not found within parameters established either by the Talmud or the supposed standard legal code with its myriads of commentaries.

Supporters of the Ashkenazi approach see it as a strength rather than a weakness. Yes, the Talmud frequently offers differing solutions to the same question, but there is a certain logic to its methodology. Admittedly, the Talmud discusses some things in an on-topic and off-topic manner. If the on-topic discussion and the off-topic discussion cannot be harmonized, the "superior explanation" follows the on-topic discussion. A clarifying example can be found in the Talmud's discussion of the direction one must face when praying. The Talmud addresses this issue once in the course of its general discussions of prayer (Tractate Berachot) and once again in the course of discussing financial law (Tractate Bava Kamma). Clearly, the better of these two Talmudic sources, the "superior explanation," is the one that explicitly discusses the direction of prayer in the context of prayer laws and rules that one should face Jerusalem while praying.[49]

The notion that even ambiguous texts have superior and inferior readings is important in conceptualizing how to approach Jewish law. The Talmud often presents us with a certain amount of textual ambiguity, and this

---

48. The Rama wrote a series of glosses to the *Shulchan Aruch* to reflect standard Ashkenazi practice, as the *Shulchan Aruch* was weighted towards the Sephardim. These glosses have been reprinted in almost every edition since then and are introduced in the text usually with a font change and the word הגה ("gloss").

49. Both Maimonides and *Tosafot* accept this as normative *halakha*.

has led scholars to wrestle for centuries with which is the superior reading of the text and which is the inferior reading. Consequently, one of the basic starting points in Jewish law is to put all the relevant texts together and read them. Once they are read, the reader ought to present all possible explanations of the text, explore the strengths and weaknesses of the different possible explanations of the text, and then come to some conclusions about the superior reading.

Perhaps there is also a bit of theology underlying the Ashkenazi take on Jewish law. It is as if they understood the Talmud's fluid approach to reaching a resolution to a legal issue as a religious ideal. How so? This multiplicity of right answers to most issues begs the question, if God has a single right answer to the issue at hand, why would God (or at the very least the great sages of the Talmud) have not revealed the single right answer to us?

American law never contemplates such theologically driven questions, and frankly, neither do the Sephardim, who maintain that one need merely to read (and if necessary, re-read) the Talmud and use it to reach a definite conclusion. If that one solution escapes those deciding the law, they just need to study harder to ascertain the single right answer. That is certainly how the Rif and Maimonides viewed the Talmud.

PRACTICAL IMPLICATIONS

Foundational texts and their binding nature shape and guide the actions of those who decide the law. In the American legal system, judges fill this niche. They preside over trials and maintain order. They review whether or not there are any illegality issues per the evidence submitted. Judges provide instructions to juries prior to their deliberations, and, in the case of bench trials, judges must decide the facts of the case and make a ruling. Judges are also responsible for sentencing convicted criminal defendants.

At the federal level, from district courts up to the US Supreme Court, judges have the final say on issues that have an effect on the lives of every American, including basic civil rights, religious freedoms, voting rights, affirmative action, and in some cases, life or death. They lead court proceedings, use established laws and guidance to determine sentencing, and rule on the constitutionality of various laws and legal precedents.[50]

The American Bar Association describes it much more colloquially:

---

50. "The Role of Judges."

Different Notions of Foundational Texts

> Judges are like umpires in baseball or referees in football or basketball. Their role is to see that the rules of court procedures are followed by both sides. Like the ump, they call 'em as they see 'em, according to the facts and law—without regard to which side is popular (no home field advantage), without regard to who is "favored," without regard for what the spectators want, and without regard to whether the judge agrees with the law.[51]

Not surprisingly, those who decide matters of Jewish law operate very differently. Traditional legalist theorists sometimes think that religious decision-makers are just faithfully applying black and white rules that govern every situation. However, even a cursory read through the *Shulchan Aruch* reveals that there are often gray areas left in purposefully for the decision-maker to assess in context. The reason for this is because every legal system needs flexibility to work.[52]

Consider this practical example. While one would never label something non-kosher as kosher, depending on the time of day on Friday before Shabbat, the expense and hardship involved, the financial situation or status of the person asking, and a hundred other variables, one may label something that is marginally kosher as permitted.[53] Without these extenuating circumstances, a lay person might think that this is a black and white issue. However, one well versed in the sources would know that the question might involve a disputed position in the Talmud or even in the Codes.[54] A onetime reliance on a previously discarded or minority position in a situation of great need might thus be permitted when a competent authority deems it appropriate. This is not to say that these broad considerations are outside of the halachic framework; these are in fact intrinsically built into the very nature of the halachic system.[55]

Another defining characteristic of Jewish law are its different categories of decision makers.

In American law, decision makers are often all called by one generic name, judge, even though there are many different types of judges.[56] So

---

51. "Courts and Legal Procedure."

52. Broyde and Goldfeder, "The Behavior of Jewish Judges."

53. For examples of such considerations, see *Shulchan Aruch Yoreh Deah* 68:11, 69:6, 113:9.

54. In contrast, flexibility in common derives from the fact that the judge can in theory prospectively change hitherto undisputed rules.

55. Broyde and Goldfeder, "The Behavior of Jewish Judges," 64.

56. For a complete listing of the different types of federal and state judges, see Gordon,

too, in Jewish law, Jewish legal decision-makers are also often all called by one generic name (rabbi). However, they do very different things and are subject to very different pressures.

There are four major categories of Jewish legal decision-makers, each possessing their own decision-making style. They are *morei hora'ah* (communal decisors), *poskim* (halachic adjudicators), *dayanim* (rabbinic court judges), and *gedolim* (literally, "great ones").[57] While there is definitely some overlap (*gedolim* are sometimes also great *poskim*, and *dayanim* might also serve as *morei hora'ah*), in general these different forms of Jewish law adjudicators serve very different communal functions and are subject to different kinds of motivations, outside influences, and concerns.[58]

Much like secular judges, their Jewish counterparts play a foundational role in the day-to-day functioning in their legal system. However, unlike the decisions of secular judges, whose rulings are binding not just for those involved in a particular case, but for all who abide by the rules of the legal system, the decisions of Jewish law adjudicators are not necessary binding for anyone other than those seeking the decision. A well-known dispute involving milk makes this point very clear.

Concerns about milk appear in many of Judaism's foundational texts. The Mishnah states that milk of a non-Jew is forbidden.[59] According to the Talmudic sages, this is due to a concern that milk from a non-kosher animal was mixed in. Later sources[60] hold that even if there is no concern of non-kosher milk getting mixed into the milk, it is still forbidden.[61] These sources imply that the requirement to drink only *chalav yisrael* (milk that has been supervised by Jews during the milking process) was instituted as a rabbinic decree (based on the principle of *lo plug*[62]) and was to be followed

---

"Types of Judges in State and Federal Judiciary—Explained."

57. The term *gedolim* typically refers to rabbinic community Jewish law and policy leaders. Sometimes, these are the most revered rabbis in a generation, presumed by many to have some measure of divine intuition in their decision-making that is not vouchsafed to others. Broyde and Goldfeder, "The Behavior of Jewish Judges," 65.

58. Broyde and Goldfeder, "The Behavior of Jewish Judges," 65.

59. Avoda Zara 35b.

60. Bet Yosef 115:1 quoting the Mordechai Avoda Zara 826 who quotes the Rabbenu Peretz and the Sma"k (an abridged version of the Sma"g which includes additional agaddic and ethical material).

61. Sh"t Rashi 152 writes that even if you know that there's no non-kosher animal in his flock his milk is forbidden.

62. When the sages instituted *takonot* (enactments) or *gezeirot* (Rabbinic decrees),

Different Notions of Foundational Texts

even if the rationale cited by the Talmud for originally instituting this requirement no longer applies.

Fast forward to our times.

In the 1950s, Rabbi Moshe Feinstein penned a groundbreaking responsum[63] in which he argued that there was room for leniency vis-à-vis the requirement of *chalav yisrael*.[64] Rabbi Feinstein's argued the following. According to the Talmud, if a Jewish watchperson sits outside a farm and, as long as the gentile farmer remains fearful that the watchperson might stand up at any moment to monitor the milking process, the milk is deemed kosher, despite the lack of uninterrupted supervision. Rabbi Feinstein felt that there is an analogous situation in the United States, due to governmental regulations prohibiting the mixture of non-cow milk with cow milk. Gentile farmers are fearful of being caught should they mix the two together. Doing so could well result in a fine or even the loss of their license. Therefore, posited Rabbi Feinstein, there is an *"anan sahadi,"* the presence of "virtual witnesses," based on the universal knowledge that the farmers are fearful of violating the law. Just as it is considered sufficient supervision according to Jewish law for a Jewish watchperson to sit outside the dairy farm even though the supervisor may never actually stand up to watch the milking process.

Why is this relevant to our discussion of binding and non-binding rulings? It's simple. If any twentieth century Torah scholar met the definition of a *gadol*, it was Rabbi Feinstein. He was the leading halachic authority of his generation, in part due to his adherence to the methods of keen analysis of legal concepts taught in the pre-World War II yeshivot of Lithuania,

---

they would use the principle of *lo plug* ("we make no distinction"), grouping all possible situations under a single model, without considering case-by-case *psak* (ruling). This form of "unified" *halakha* bolsters the acceptance of the *gezeirah* by all individuals. "The Laws of Lo Plug."

63. *Igrot Moshe, Yoreh Deah* 1:47.

64. Truth be told, most American Jews were drinking what Rabbi Feinstein called "chalav hacompanies" well before he issued is famous ruling and even long before he arrived in America in 1937. American Jews turned to respected rabbis who had already ruled it was permissible, such as R' Dov Revel, R' Yisrael Avraham Abba Krieger, R' Breuer, R' Moshe Soloveitchik and his son R' Joseph B. Soloveitchik. Quite tellingly, in the early days of Lakewood, home to a very prominent and very strict yeshiva community, they served regular milk and Breakstone cottage cheese. That stopped when *chalav yisrael* became more readily available, but clearly the yeshiva would not have served "chalav hacompanies" had their *Rosh Yeshiva* R' Aharon Kotler believed *chalav yisrael* was mandatory.

where they emphasized legal theory rather than its application in practice. He published commentaries on a number of Talmudic tractates, but his fame rests chiefly on his collections of responsa under the name *Iggerot Moshe*, "Letters of Moses." His decisions in these responsa are widely held to be authoritative for the whole world of Orthodoxy.[65]

If any rabbinic rulings issued over the past hundred years should be binding, it ought to be Rabbi Feinstein's. Yet, we know that a significant portion of the Orthodox world rejected his ruling on *chalav yisrael*. Some thought he was too lenient. Others disputed the fact upon which the responsa was based, arguing that government regulations and fear of legal consequences cannot be equated to the credibility of two witnesses.[66] Still others maintain that in places where *chalav yisrael* is readily available at prices not significantly higher than regular milk, it is not appropriate for anyone to rely on Rabbi Feinstein's leniency.[67]

In short, while many Orthodox Jews are comfortable drinking the milk they purchase in their local grocery stores, a significant segment of the Orthodox world continues to insist on *chalav yisrael*. Rabbi Feinstein's ruling is in theory foundational, but it is far from binding.

Imagine what would happen in America if people refused to see court decisions as binding. Actually, we know what would happen because it has happened.

In 2015, Kim Davis, then a Kentucky county clerk, cited her religious beliefs in refusing to issue marriage licenses to same-sex couples, notwithstanding the Supreme Court's ruling that same year that the fundamental right to marry is guaranteed to same-sex couples by both the Due Process Clause and the Equal Protection Clause of the Fourteenth Amendment of the Constitution.[68] Davis argued that her actions were protected by the First Amendment. Her arguments were rebuffed unanimously by the three-judge panel of the United States Court of Appeals for the Sixth Circuit that

---

65. My Jewish Learning, Moshe Feinstein

66. Heinemann, "Cholov Yisroel."

67. Additional questions and concerns have arisen due to a 2017 governmental revision of what constitute Grade "A" pasteurized milk. Per that revision, "milk" now can mean not only milk from kosher animals such as cows and goats, but even milk from "other hooved animals" such as camels. (See Section 4, paragraph 3 of the Grade "A" Pasteurized Milk Ordinance, and the Definition of "Hooved Mammals' Milk" in Section 1.) This has led some to question the basic premise of Rabbi Feinstein's leniency. Reiss, "Camels, Cows and Chalav Certification."

68. *Obergefell v. Hodges*, 576 U.S. 644 (2015).

Different Notions of Foundational Texts

declared, "It cannot be defensibly argued that the holder of the Rowan County clerk's office... may decline to act in conformity with the United States Constitution."[69]

Davis appealed to the US Supreme Court, but the Court declined to hear her case. She defied the courts and continued not to issue marriage licenses to same-sex couples. As a result, she was jailed for contempt of court. She also lost her 2018 bid to be reelected as county clerk. Ultimately, one of the couples denied a marriage license by Davis sued her, and, in 2024, Davis was ordered by a federal judge to pay a total of $260,104 in fees and expenses to attorneys who represented the couple, plus an additional $100,000 in damages to the couple themselves.[70]

---

69. Adam Liptak, "Supreme Court Says Kentucky Clerk Must Let Gay Couples Marry."

70. "A former clerk who refused to issue marriage licenses must pay $260,000 in fees and costs, a judge rules." US News, "A Former Clerk Who Refused to Issue Marriage Licenses Must Pay $260,000 in Fees and Costs, a Judge Rules."

CHAPTER FOUR

Underlying Expectations

IN 1977, THE *MICHIGAN Law Review* ran an article that I think makes an astute observation:

> Any mandatory legal rule is bound to encounter some noncompliance, which may arise not only from deliberate disobedience but also from such sources as lapse of rationality, weakness of will, inattentiveness, ignorance, and mistake. Noncompliance due to sources other than deliberate disobedience is generally not responsive to increases in enforcement and severity of penalties, and it thus seems clear that at least some noncompliance is inevitable.[1]

Given this reality, the question to be asked is, what are the expectations of Jewish law and secular law regarding noncompliance? Do these legal systems differentiate between "deliberate disobedience" and "lapses or rationality" or "mistakes," and if so, how? More importantly, what are the expectations of each system in terms of the "law breaker"? Is the goal that law breakers learn from their mistakes and perhaps even feel remorseful about their behavior? Or is it merely a matter of increasingly severe consequences so as to constrain and deter inappropriate or unlawful behaviors? In answering such questions, we will see that Jewish law differs significantly from American law in three areas: whether lawbreakers are to be incarcerated, the weight given to the circumstances underlying unlawful or sinful behavior, and the preference for repentance rather than punishment.

1. "Laws That Are Made to Be Broken: Adjusting for Anticipated Noncompliance."

Underlying Expectations

In biblical times, when there was a full functional Jewish judiciary, incarceration was not part of the legal paradigm, but capital punishment was, at least in theory. The Torah specifically mandates the death penalty for thirty-six offenses, including murder, kidnapping, adultery, incest, certain forms of rape, idolatrous worship, public incitement to apostasy, and publicly desecrating the Sabbath. In reality, the Talmudic sages effectively legislated capital punishment out of existence, as they famously said: "A Sanhedrin that executes [a transgressor] once in seven years is characterized as destructive. Rabbi Elazar ben Azarya says: once in seventy years. Rabbi Tarfon and Rabbi Akiva say: If we had been [members] of the Sanhedrin, no person would have ever been executed."[2]

In addition to murder, the Torah recognizes that unintentional killings, what would be termed homicides in American law, are sadly part of daily life. Anticipating this, the Torah decreed the establishment of "cities of refuge."[3] The cities functioned as follows. The perpetrator of a homicide would flee to one of the designated cities of refuge immediately following the death of the victim in order to avoid being killed by the avenger. In the Torah, it states that the victim's next of kin is permitted to avenge the wrongful death.[4] At this point, agents of the court would return the perpetrator under escort to the locale where the incident took place to face judgment. If the court found it to be an act of murder, the perpetrator faced execution (although, as we have noted, the likelihood of execution was nil). If the court determined that the homicide was the result of a freak accident, totally unforeseeable by anyone, the perpetrator would be exonerated and allowed to return to normal life. However, if the homicide was the result of some degree of negligence, the perpetrator would be forced to flee once again to a city of refuge to avoid being killed by the avenger, who still had the right to kill him.

Other acts of violence, such as assault, were to be punished financially. Jewish law requires five distinct types of reparation in cases of assault: actual damages or financial loss suffered by the victim, pain inflicted upon the victim, medical expenses incurred by the victim, compensation of any lost wages resulting for the victim's injuries, and any embarrassment felt by the

---

2. Mishnah Makkot 1:10

3. Numbers 35:10–12.

4. "But if the killer ever goes outside the limits of the city of refuge to which he has fled, and the blood-avenger comes upon him outside the limits of his city of refuge, and the blood-avenger kills the killer, there is no bloodguilt on his account." Numbers 35:26–27.

victim because of the assault.[5] There is no incarceration, nor would there be in cases of theft. Rich or poor, a regular thief pays double indemnity. If, however, the thief stole an ox or sheep, a four- or fivefold payment is demanded, as the verse states: "If a man steals an ox or sheep and slaughters or sells it, five oxen shall he pay for the ox, and four sheep for the sheep."[6]

In terms of illegal activities, such as murder or theft, circumstances do not matter in Jewish law. However, when it comes to ritual issues or activities deemed sinful, circumstances do matter. The sages recognized that different factors and motivations can underlie different sins. Unlike American law, where circumstances might matter when it comes to sentencing but typically not when determining guilt, Jewish law takes intentionality into account. It also considers what motivates an individual to act when establishing categories of sinful behavior.

The Talmud explicitly speaks of two distinct types of sinners. The first, referred to as a *mumar lete'avon* or an "involuntary apostate" in English, is one who, in order to satisfy some physical desire, habitually transgresses one of the Torah's injunctions. The Talmudic sages understood that such people are not rebelling by their sinful conduct. They simply cannot control their desires or impulses. The sages did not condone this sinful conduct. Rather, they viewed it as an involuntary exception to a lifestyle otherwise in accordance with Jewish law and practice.

This is a far cry from the second type of sinner discussed by the Talmud. This individual, called a *mumar le'hachis* or a "true apostate" in English, is viewed quite unfavorably, for he or she is motivated not by gratification of desire, but by sheer rebellious spite. It is not that they cannot control their actions. They simply choose not to and thus embrace their sinful conduct as a rebuke to or a denial of God.

Jewish law further differentiates between types of sinful behavior by introducing the concept of "light" sins and "severe" sins. There is much discussion in the rabbinic literature on this topic, but it is Maimonides who gives us the simplest explanation. He maintains that the severity of a sin is reflected by the punishment proscribed by the Torah for such actions. Hence, severe sins are those for which one is liable for *karet*, that is, execution by the court. Light sins encompass all other prohibitions or the failure to perform positive commandments that are not punishable by *karet*.[7]

---

5. Mishnah Bava Kamma 8:1.
6. Exodus 21:37.
7. *Mishneh Torah*, Laws of Repentance 1:2.

Underlying Expectations

In their discussions of sin, the Talmudic sages consistently focus on the conduct of the individual and not on the individual themselves. To illustrate the difference, consider a Jew who regularly eats pork, which many view as the most non-kosher of foods. Jewish law categorizes one who eats pork as sinful. Nonetheless, Jewish law has no category called "pork eaters," regardless of how many individuals in the community eat it.

There is one final puzzle piece for us to consider if we are to arrive at a full understanding of how the Jewish legal tradition addresses sinful behavior. It is the question of where sinful behavior takes place: in private or in public.

There is a fascinating story in Moed Katan (17a) that sheds light on the notion of private versus public sins. The Talmud tells us of a certain Torah scholar whose scholarship was widely respected but whose reputation had been sullied by rumors concerning his sexual misdeeds. Rav Yehuda maintained that this scholar should be excommunicated. The sages disagreed because they felt his teachings benefited the community. In the end, Rav Yehuda prevailed and ostracized the man. After Rav Yehuda's death, the scholar pleaded with the sages to restore him to his former standing in the community. The sages considered his circumstances as well as prior precedents before them and ultimately denied his request. The ostracized scholar died shortly thereafter in a tragic, yet bizarre manner that made clear to the sages the validity of the rumors about his inappropriate and sinful behavior.[8] What was less clear was where and how this scholar should be buried.

Because he was a great Torah scholar, his body was initially taken to the caves where pious individuals were interred. However, as the text relates, the caves did not accept him. A snake stood at the entrance of the caves and did not let them pass. Those tasked with burying the body then went to the caves of the judges, where the heads of the courts, whose status was less than the pious one, were buried. Those caves accepted him. The Gemara asks why the body was rejected by the first caves and accepted by the second. Here is the answer given:

> Even though he sinned, he still acted in accordance with the opinion of Rabbi Ilai, as it is taught in a *baraita*: Rabbi Ilai says: If a person sees that his evil inclination is gaining control over him and he cannot overcome it, then he should go to a place where he is not known. He should wear black, and he should wrap his head

---

8. According to the Talmud, a wasp came and stung him on his penis, and he died.

> in black, as if he were a mourner. Perhaps these changes will influence him, so that he not sin. Even if these actions do not help, he should at least do as his heart desires in private and not desecrate the name of Heaven in public.[9]

How are we to understand this story? Since he is unknown in his new locale, his sinful behavior will not cause a desecration of God's name. In a sense, this relocation is akin to sinning in private because it does not, in the words of the Talmud, "desecrate the name of Heaven in public."

The earliest Jewish legal authorities carefully considered this imperative not to desecrate God's name in public and drew three distinctions. The first was that one who engages in sinful conduct that is common behavior in the broader community is not considered an apostate. This also holds true for improper beliefs commonly found in the broader community. Rather, the individual ought to be viewed as an accidental sinner.

The second view disagrees and maintains that even gross and consistent violations of Jewish law, if done in private or unintentionally, are never grounds for exclusion from the Jewish community. The approach does not deny the sinful nature of these acts, even when committed in private. It instead holds that such actions are typically driven by desire, and thus the sinner falls under the rubric of a *mumar lete'avon*, that is, an "involuntary apostate."

The third approach is put forward by Maimonides. For him, the core issue does not center on the question of public versus private misbehavior. It is all a matter of faith. Does the individual lack faith generally in Jewish law or in the specific law he or she violates? In either case, Maimonides believes that a lack of faith is grounds for shunning the individual or removing the person from the community.[10] Said differently, per Maimonides, an "involuntary apostate" is never cut off by the community. Only one lacking in faith is cut off, even if this lack of faith is limited to a particular set of circumstances or a specific *halakha*.[11]

The third and most important difference between Jewish and American law centers on the issue of repentance versus punishment. Repentance,

---

9. Moed Katan 17a.

10. Some beliefs are so core and central to Judaism that even private or unintentional violations are grounds to expel of shun the individual. These include the belief that God is corporeal and the belief in more than one deity.

11. The *Shulchan Aruch* codifies this view in Yoreh De'ah 2:5: "An (true) apostate, even against one Jewish law ... [has] the status of non-Jews."

or *teshuva* as it is known in Hebrew, is a highly valued concept in Judaism, so much so that, according to the oral tradition, it one of the seven things that were formed before the world was created.[12] Repentance plays a necessary and twofold role in Jewish law, as explained by the Rav, Rabbi Soloveitchik. A wrong committed against another produces a liability on the part of the perpetrator vis-à-vis the victim. The Rav maintains that to counter this culpability, the perpetrator must make restitution or financial compensation, and this in turn brings about a form of forgiveness or acquittal from wrongdoing.[13] Thus, an individual who undertakes this kind of *teshuva* both literally and metaphorically pays a debt owed to another and is thereby released from further liability.[14]

In the Rav's view, repentance plays a second and equally important role. Wrongdoing is accompanied by the impurity of sin which, in turn, imparts spiritual defilement. Hence, says the Rav, the individual must do more than merely pay the victim any restitution arising out of the wrongdoing. Reparation alone is insufficient. It must be accompanied by penance in the form of fundamental change in the individual's mode of behavior. This is reflected in Maimonides's Laws of Repentance, when he notes the practice of changing one's name after undergoing the process of *teshuva*, to demonstrate that "I am someone else, not the person who committed the wrongful."[15] Is it any wonder that the Talmudic sages declare: "In the place where penitents (*baal teshuva*) stand, even the full-fledged righteous (*tzadik gamur*) do not stand."[16]

Equally unsurprising is the fact that the sages would craft legal requirements in a manner that would facilitate repentance on the part of the wrongdoer. For instance, in discussing a series of cases in which thief effected a physical change to a stolen item (such as turning a stolen hide into a finished good or using a stolen beam to construct a new house), the

---

12. The other seven are the Torah itself, Gehinnom (a term generally used to describe the place of torment reserved for the wicked after death), the Garden of Eden, God's Throne of Glory, the Temple, and the Name of the Messiah. Pirkei DeRabbi Eliezer 3:3–4.

13. Levine, "Teshuva."

14. Interestingly, the Rav notes an etymological link that underscores the corresponding conceptual similarity between reparation and this form of forgiveness. He notes that the Hebrew word for atonement, *kappara*, derives from the same root as *kofer*, the Hebrew term for payment of an obligation.

15. *Mishneh Torah*, Laws of Repentance 2:4.

16. Talmud Bavli Berakhot 34b.

sages explicitly ruled that the thief not be ordered to demolish the house to return the beam itself. Their rationale? To encourage robbers to admit their crime, repent, and then reimburse the owner for the stolen item.[17]

How different is the thrust of the American judicial system, which has increasingly been built upon the notions of punishment and incarceration? After decades of stability from the 1920s to the early 1970s, the rate of imprisonment in the United States more than quadrupled in the last four decades. The US penal population of 2.2 million adults is by far the largest in the world. Just under one-quarter of the world's prisoners are held in American prisons. The US rate of incarceration, with nearly one out of every hundred adults in prison or jail, is five to ten times higher than the rates in Western Europe and other democracies.[18]

How does this translate to day-to-day life in America? On any given day, about two million people in the US are locked up in jails, prisons, and other spaces of confinement. More significantly, half of all Americans have an immediate family member who has been incarcerated. One in five people have had a parent incarcerated, and 2.6 million children have a parent who is currently incarcerated.[19]

Given these numbers, we must ask a very obvious question. What impact does America's reliance on incarceration have on its crime rate? Answering this is complicated. First, because, as people who work with data know, numbers can be manipulated and crunched in countless ways. Thus, it can be challenging to arrive at a straightforward answer. Moreover, discussions of crime rates in America today have become a highly politicized topic, with each side positing diametrically different conclusions, as documented by a 2023 Gallup survey. According to Gallup, 92 percent of Republicans believe that crime is rising, compared to 58 percent of Democrats.[20]

The truth is, both groups are wrong. Let's take a look at the historical data from 1990 to 2022.[21] Murders per 100,000 people hit a peak of 9.8 in 1991. They have dropped in every subsequent year, reaching a low of 4.5 in

---

17. The sages reach make this determination in multiple cases. See Talmud Bavli Bava Kamma 66b, 94a, 94b, and 95a.

18. Travis, Western, and Redburn, eds., Exploring Causes and Consequences."

19. Widra, "Ten statistics about the scale and impact of mass incarceration in the US."

20. The same poll indicates that 78 percent of independents believe that crime is on the rise. Dilanian, "Most People Think the US Crime Rate is Rising. They're Wrong."

21. These data are set forth in the most recent annual crime report published by the Federal Bureau of Investigation in October 2023.

2013 and again in 2014 (a decline of 54 percent). They subsequently rose each year and peaked in 2020 and 2021 at 6.8 (an increase of 51 percent). In 2022, they dropped to 6.3.

Alarming as these figures seem at first glance, criminal justice professionals are often able to demonstrate links between social problems and illegal activity. This was certainly true during the COVID-19 pandemic, when the negative effects of this global health crisis on social connections, physical health, mental health, and the economy were quite apparent. Many point to COVID as the single most significant underlying cause of the recent spike in murder rates. It was also evident in the 9.2 percent increase in auto theft during the pandemic.

Compounding matters, the earliest reports on crime during the height of the pandemic came from media outlets that conducted their own surface-level data analyses. According to a research review published by the *American Journal of Criminal Justice*, media outlets often used an unreliable variety of data and anecdotal evidence in their reporting. Media outlets like *The Washington Post* and CNN were further criticized for utilizing limited metrics to compare early-pandemic crime rates to those in previous weeks, months, and years. Their reports showed increases in crime rates, which was inconsistent with other data indicating that crime, overall, was exhibiting a downward trend.[22] For instance, violent crimes per 100,000 people was falling steadily, even during the pandemic. In 1990, the rate was 729.6. In 2022, it was down to 369.8 (a decline of 49 percent). Non-violent crimes fell even more sharply. Property crimes per 100,000 people were at 5,073.1 in 1990 and dipped to 1,954.4 in 2022 (a decline of 61 percent).

Are these declines due to the burgeoning incarceration rate in the US? Apparently not. Despite its widespread use, research shows that the effect of incarceration as a deterrent to crime is minimal at best and has been diminishing for several years. Indeed, increased rates of incarceration have had no demonstrated effect on violent crime. In some instances it may even increase crime (a point we will return to shortly).[23]

Yet, even if we were to assume that high incarceration rates did serve as a deterrent to crime, most people would be dismissive of this idea. Consider the table below. Crime was down nationally in the two-year period from 2020 to 2022. It was dramatically down in some major cities, such

---

22. "How COVID-19 Changed Crime in the US."
23. "The Prison Paradox: More Incarceration Will Not Make Us Safer."

as Chicago and Baltimore, but spiked in others, such as New Orleans, San Francisco, and Los Angeles.

Recent Changes in Crime Rates in Selected Major Cities, 2020-2022

	Murders Per 100,000 (2022)	Change In Murder Rate (2020-22)
National	6.3	−6.7%
New York	5.3	−5.7%
Los Angeles	10.2	15.8%
Chicago	22.8	−20.4%
Houston	19	11.6%
Philadelphia*	33	7.3%
San Francisco	7.2	32.1%
Baltimore*	50.3	−11.8%
Washington, DC	29.3	5.6%
Atlanta*	33.9	7.7%
Detroit	49.1	−1.2%
New Orleans	71.9	40.8%
Memphis	43	−3.0%
Seattle	7.4	9.8%

Note: Cities indicated with an asterisk were not listed in the FBI's 2020 report. Murder counts for that year were obtained from other sources. Violent crime and property crime estimates for these cities will be added later after careful review of the data. Percentage changes were calculated from raw unrounded figures.

Source: FBI Uniform Crime Reporting Program, 2020 and 2022, Tables 1 and 8.

An individual's perception of crime being up or down is clearly influenced by geography. However, there is more at play here. According to criminologist Jeff Asher, who analyzed the FBI numbers, there is no way to counter the idea that "crime is rising." As he notes, "It's just an overwhelming number of news media stories and viral videos—I have to believe that social media is playing a role."[24] In short, people tend to believe what they see and hear, and the messaging on crime rates does not correlate to the facts.

---

24. Dilanian, "Most People Think the US Crime Rate is Rising. They're Wrong."

Underlying Expectations

The effectiveness of incarceration is undercut by another reality. Locking criminals up may well provide punishment. It certainly sequesters them away from public life for a time. However, that may be all it does. A large body of research finds that spending time in prison or jail does not lower the risk that someone will offend again.[25] It actually increases the likelihood that those who are incarcerated will commit future crimes.[26] Factually speaking, recidivism rates in the US are some of the highest in the world, with almost 44 percent of released criminals returning to prison within their first year out.[27]

There is one final factor that brings into question the wisdom of America's high incarceration rates, a concept known as "mass incarceration." At its most basic level, it is a term often used to describe the exceedingly high rate of incarceration in the United States for both adults and youths. However, in 2010, the term took on new connotations with the publication of Michelle Alexander's *The New Jim Crow*.[28] Her book, whose title harkens back to one of the most racist periods in US history, sparked many debates and brought new attention to the over-incarceration of people of color. To wit, while people of color make up about 30 percent of the United States population, they account for 60 percent of those imprisoned.[29]

Before digging deeper into Alexander's basic premises[30] and their implications for our understanding of the overarching goals of American

25. Cruz, "Rethinking Prison as a Deterrent to Future Crime."

26. Bryant, "Why Punishing People in Jail and Prison Isn't Working."

27. Criminon International, "Nine States Have Reduced Their Prisoner Population by 30%."

28. Alexander, *The New Jim Crow*.

29. "Mass Incarceration & People of Color."

30. There was, to be sure, criticism of Alexander's proposition even in the Black community. For instance, James Forman Jr. an Afro-American American legal scholar who serves as the J. Skelly Wright Professor of Law at Yale Law School, argues that Alexander's Jim Crow analogy obscures much that matters in the analysis of origins of America's mass incarceration. He maintains that the Jim Crow analogy has too little to say about Black people's attitudes toward crime and punishment, which masks the nature and extent of the Black community's support for punitive crime policy. He also explains how what he calls the Jim Crow analogy's myopic focus on the "War on Drugs" diverts society's focus from violent crimes, which destroys so many lives in low-income Black communities. Forman further argues that the Jim Crow analogy obscures the fact that mass incarceration's impact has been almost exclusively concentrated among the most disadvantaged African-Americans, and it takes attention away from the harms that mass incarceration inflicts on other racial groups, including Whites and Hispanics. Forman Jr., "Racial Critiques of Mass Incarceration."

law, we must digress and examine some relevant case histories from the Supreme Court.

As the subtitle of Alexander's book (*Mass Incarceration in the Age of Colorblindness*) suggests, the interaction between the law and mass incarceration in the modern era has been complicated and at times misdirected. This is borne out by several important Supreme Court rulings that address the anti-discrimination protections inherent in the Equal Protection Clause of the Fourteenth Amendment to the US Constitution.

The first of these is the 1976 Supreme Court decision in *Washington v. Davis*.[31] That decision led to the establishment of the "Intent Standard," which requires plaintiffs to prove a perpetrator's discriminatory "intent" in order to prove an anti-discrimination claim. In other words, facts, no matter the extent to which they seem to demonstrate discrimination, count for little if an intent to discriminate on the part of the defendant cannot be proven. Moreover, contemporary discrimination is frequently structural in nature, unconscious, or sometimes hidden behind pretexts (despite the fact that a tangible harm has resulted from their actions). Hence, the showing of "intent" is a near impossible burden for plaintiffs.[32]

Unfortunately, *Washington* was only the beginning, and in the years that followed, the Supreme Court expanded the Intent Standard's reach into almost all equal protection cases. For instance, in 1980, the Court applied the intent requirement to an area that had traditionally been accorded the greatest constitutional respect: voting.[33] This decision greatly enhanced the burden of proof in that area and represented a major obstacle to successful litigation.[34] Then, in 1987, the Court imposed the Intent Standard on challenges to death sentences, almost entirely preventing capital defendants from raising the issue of race in their defense.[35] Finally, in 2001, the Court employed the standard to prevent private plaintiffs from using Title VI to seek redress for institutional, structural, and systemic discrimination promulgated by institutions receiving federal funds.[36]

The notion of proving "intent" has also bled into areas of law outside of equal protection jurisprudence. In recent years, courts have demanded

---

31. *Washington v. Davis*, 426 U.S. 229 (1976).
32. Equal Justice Society, "Intent Doctrine."
33. *Mobile v. Bolden*, 446 U.S. 55 (1980).
34. Rinehart, "Proving Intentional Discrimination in Equal Protection Cases."
35. *McCleskey v. Kemp*: 481 U.S. 279 (1987).
36. *Alexander v. Sandoval*: 532 U.S. 275 (2001).

that plaintiffs prove "intent" in education, employment, criminal law, and environmental cases. Consequently, protection against any form of discrimination is constrained and deterred and likely will be as long as the requirement to prove intent remains in place.[37]

The relevancy of these decisions to debates surrounding the mass incarceration of disproportionate numbers of people of color should be apparent. While these cases make it difficult to argue in a court setting that mass incarceration in America is discriminatory and racially driven, the facts do speak for themselves, as Alexander demonstrates time and again in her book. She traces the beginning of this to the Reagan Administration's "war on drugs," which began in 1982. Her contention is that, while the initiative was framed as a drug war, it had far more to do with race than anything else.

When this war on drugs was launched, even conservatives in Reagan's own party were skeptical. It seemed like a solution looking for a problem. Fortunately for its proponents, the problem presented itself in 1985, when crack cocaine appeared in poor, Black neighborhoods, leading to a major spike in violence and drug use. Crack cocaine and the violence it inspired was a convenient way to justify a war on drugs, and, in response, the DEA ramped up its public awareness efforts, drawing attention to the "new" crack problem. The media joined in the chorus of outrage and played up the characterizations. "Thousands of stories about the crack crisis flooded the airwaves and newsstands, and the stories had a clear racial subtext. The articles typically featured black "crack whores," "crack babies," and "gang-bangers," reinforcing already prevalent racial stereotypes of black women as irresponsible, selfish "welfare queens," and black men as 'predators'—part of an inferior and criminal subculture."[38]

Yet, in Alexander's view, the strongest evidence of the discriminatory nature of the war on drugs was the 1986 Anti-Drug Abuse Act. This act created a scientifically unjustifiable 100-to-1 crack versus powder cocaine sentencing disparity under which distribution of just five grams of crack carried a minimum five-year federal prison sentence, while distribution of 500 grams of powder cocaine carried the same five-year mandatory minimum sentence. To be clear, crack cocaine and powder cocaine are two forms of the same drug, but because the majority of people arrested for crack offenses were African American, the 100:1 ratio resulted in vast

---

37. Equal Justice Society, "Intent Doctrine."
38. "Narrative Shift And The Campaign To End Racial Profiling."

racial disparities in the average length of sentences for comparable offenses. On average, under the 100:1 regime, African Americans served virtually as much time in prison for non-violent drug offenses as whites did for violent offenses.[39]

In 2010, Congress passed the Fair Sentencing Act, which reduced the sentencing disparity between offenses for crack and powder cocaine from 100:1 to 18:1, but the damage had already been done. According to Human Rights Watch, people of color were no more likely to use or sell illegal drugs than whites, but they had higher rate of arrests. Thus, while African Americans comprised 14 percent of regular drug users, they accounted for 37 percent of those arrested for drug offenses. In addition, African Americans were 21 percent more likely to receive mandatory-minimum sentences than white defendants and were 20 percent more like to be sentenced to prison. The net result? From 1980 to 2007, about one in three of the 25.4 million adults arrested for drugs was African American.[40]

For our purposes, the question of intentionality is not particularly relevant. Whether mass incarceration is deliberatively discriminatory or not, it highlights the extent to which American law's reliance on punishment and imprisonment is flawed and unfair.

In the final analysis, it is impossible to draw conclusions as to which legal system has the better approach to stemming lawlessness. There is neither evidence nor data to tell us about crime rates in biblical Israel. The Talmudic sages teach that the First Temple was destroyed because the Jewish society of that time was steeped in murder. Does this prove that Judaism's emphasis on repentance was ineffective in deterring crime? Not necessarily, because these very same sages also said that illicit sexual relations and idol worship were equally to blame for the Temple's destruction.[41] Therefore, in lieu of conclusions, allow me to offer some observations.

American law functions in the here and now. It has fully embraced Justice Homes's bad-man theory and seeks to deter crime via punishments and incarceration. Thus, when presented with sufficient evidence, a court will find a contrite defendant just as guilty as an unrepentant one (although contrition on the part of the guilty party might result in a more lenient sentence).[42] Given the political environment we find ourselves in in 2024,

39. ACLU, "Fair Sentencing Act."
40. Keyes, "Mass Incarceration & People of Color."
41. Talmud Bavli Yoma 9b.
42. The research literature generally supports the notion that remorsefulness reduces

one in which political leaders from both parties cannot even agree on what crime data tells us, this is unlikely to change any time soon. Punishment and incarceration will continue to be seen as the correct response.

In contrast, Jewish law is concerned with both the present and the future, with life in this world and with life "in the World to Come."[43] Jewish law does not ignore criminality. It certainly delineates how those guilty of rape, assault, and murder are to be punished. Yet it also legislates things that are incomprehensible from an American law perspective because it is a theologically based legal system. Why is one not allowed to wear a garment made of wool and linen?[44] Why is one forbidden from eating a pork chop but allowed to eat a lamb chop? Even the most learned Jew cannot explain the rationale for such injunctions. Nevertheless, an observant Jew refrains from wearing wool and linen garments and from eating pork chops simply because it is God's will. This individual therefore observes the law in order to build, strengthen, and maintain a relationship with God. Doing so is not premised on punishment (even though Jewish law clearly defines the consequences of sinful behaviors). One who sins and wishes to restore a relationship with God must be remorseful, and that in turn leads to repentance.

Here then is perhaps the best way to summarize the differing approaches the Jewish and American legal systems. In America, the unrepentant go to jail whether or not they feel remorse. In Jewish law, the unrepentant remain cut off from God and are thus denied eternal life in the World to Come. As Maimonides writes in his Laws of Repentance: "Since free choice is granted to all men as explained, a person should always strive to repent and to confess verbally for his sins, striving to cleanse his hands

the severity of sentences for convicted offenders. Corwin, Cramer, Griffin and Brodsky, "Defendant Remorse, Need for Affect, and Juror Sentencing Decisions."

43. The World to Come—or *olam ha-bah* in Hebrew—is a general Jewish term for the hereafter. References to it are sprinkled throughout ancient Jewish texts, though the particulars of what it means are not entirely clear. Some understand it to refer to a heavenly abode where the souls of the righteous live on after death. Others see it as the perfected world that will follow the coming of the messiah, when the dead are resurrected, and complete peace prevails. My Jewish Learning, "The World to Come."

44. The Torah prohibits the wearing of wool and linen together in two places: Leviticus 19:19 and Deuteronomy 22:9. According to the talmudic rabbis, the prohibition set forth in these verses only applied to mixing linen made from the flax plant with wool from sheep or lambs. The rabbis worried, however, that some less-common fabrics, such as silk, might be confused for flax, and therefore prohibited mixtures involving such materials out of fear of *marit ayin*–giving the appearance of breaking a law. When silk became more common, such concerns disappeared, and later legal authorities eliminated these prohibitions (*Shulkhan Arukh Yoreh Deah* 298:1). Jacobs, What Is Shatnez?

from sin in order that he may die as a *Baal-Teshuvah* [a fully repentant individual] and merit the life of the world to come."[45]

---

45. *Mishneh Torah,* Hilchot Teshuva 7:1.

CHAPTER FIVE

Case Studies

As we have already noted, the US Constitution defines what is legal, not what is moral, and America's founders openly embraced this idea. Just take a look at the Treaty of Tripoli of 1797, which was negotiated under George Washington, approved unanimously by the US Senate, and signed by President John Adams.[1] It states quite emphatically that "[t]he government of the United States of America is not, in any sense, founded on the Christian Religion." When taken in tandem with the First Amendment, which Jefferson revered "as building a wall of separation between church and state,"[2] we see that America's founders strove to establish a secular republic ruled by democratic laws, not sectarian faith. As such, its legal system typically steers clear of issues of morality. One notable exception to this was Prohibition, which banned the manufacture, transportation, and sale of intoxicating liquors.

Driven by religiously based morality, Prohibition became the law of the land in January 1920 upon the ratification of the Eighteenth Amendment. However, the roots of Prohibition can be traced to the 1820s and 1830s, when a wave of religious revivalism swept the United States and led

---

1. The 1797 Treaty of Tripoli was just one of many similar agreements established in the period between the United States and the rulers of the North African states of Algiers, Tunis, and Tripoli to protect American sailors and shipping from attack by Barbary pirates.

2. Jefferson penned this phrase in his 1802 letter to the Danbury Baptist Association. In it, Jefferson declared that when the American people adopted the establishment clause, they built a "wall of separation between the church and state." Ryman and Alcorn, "Establishment Clause: Separation of Church and State."

to increased calls for temperance. In 1838, Massachusetts became the first state to pass a temperance law banning the sale of spirits. Maine followed suit in 1846, and by the time the Civil War began in 1861, several other states had their own temperance laws.

By the turn of the century, temperance societies were a common fixture in communities across the United States. In the face of mounting pressure, Congress in 1917 submitted the Eighteenth Amendment for state ratification. Consistent with the process of amending the US Constitution, Congress stipulated a seven-year time limit for ratification. In actuality, the process took just eleven months.

By any measure, Prohibition was a disastrous piece of legislation. It was difficult to enforce. It spurred a dramatic increase in the illegal production and sale of liquor, as well as a proliferation of illegal drinking spots. Not surprisingly, these illegal activities were accompanied by a rise in gang violence and other crimes. This led to waning support for Prohibition by the end of the 1920s, and in early 1933, Congress adopted a resolution proposing a Twenty-First Amendment to the Constitution that would repeal Prohibition. The Twenty-First Amendment was ratified even more quickly than the amendment it replaced.

State law would also from time to time try to legislate morality, but these efforts ultimately fared no better than Prohibition. Take adultery as an example. For decades, state law tried to legislate morality by making adultery a crime. In fact, up until the 1960s, prosecutions for adultery and sodomy laws were a regular feature of the legal systems in many states.[3]

While the Supreme Court has never directly ruled on the constitutionality of adultery laws, it has issued key rulings in matters of sex and privacy. An individual's right to privacy was recognized in *Griswold v. Connecticut*, where the Supreme Court held a Connecticut law restricting access to contraceptives was unconstitutional.[4] Although *Griswold* addressed a case of a married couple, the principles of *Griswold* were extended to unmarried couples on Equal Protection grounds less than a decade later in *Eisenstadt v. Baird*.[5] In 2003, the Court went even further, ruling that state laws banning homosexual sodomy were unconstitutional as a violation of the right to privacy.[6]

---

3. Echols, "Decriminalizing Adultery."
4. *Griswold v. Connecticut*, 381 U.S. 479 (1965).
5. *Eisenstadt v. Baird*, 405 U.S. 438 (1972).
6. *Lawrence v. Texas*, 539 U.S. 558 (2003).

Case Studies

What we can glean from the examples of Prohibition and adultery is that morality and legality do not work well in tandem in the American legal system.[7] More fundamentally, we see that the courts will, at some point, intervene to divorce morality from legality. In contrast, Jewish law is often about morality comingling with legality.

We have discussed this in general terms up to this point. We shall now examine a number of case studies intended to highlight how each legal systems wrestles with the notions of morality and legality. Before doing so, let's consider an example that will help put these case studies into context.

The notion of a void contract is well-established in American law. It is definitionally a purported agreement that is unenforceable from the moment it is created, and it differs from a voidable contract. While a void contract was never legally valid and will never be enforceable, voidable contracts may be valid until one party formally rejects the terms for reasons allowable in the contract or by law. Voidable contracts may also be legally enforceable once any defects in the contract are corrected.[8]

The classic example of a void contract is one that involves illegal actions. Thus, if Party A pays Party B $100 for illegal drugs, but Party B fails to deliver the drugs, Party A has no legal standing to demand that the "contract" be fulfilled. Similarly, if Party C pays Party D $100 to engage in sexual activities, there are no grounds for Party D to sue Party C for non-payment, as prostitution is illegal in every state except for Nevada.[9]

Interestingly, the Talmud addresses this very case, prostitution, in a broader discussion of the enforceability of contracts in Jewish law.

The definition of "double jeopardy" in Jewish law is very different from the concept in American law.[10] In Jewish law, should an individual simultaneously violate two biblical prohibitions, one that carries a financial penalty and another for which he might be liable for capital punishment,[11]

---

7. We should not say the law itself is morally indifferent, even though it might be true that the various principles of interpretation and application might be. Riga, "The Law and Morals."

8. Bloomenthal, "Void Contract Definition and What Happens."

9. Nevada is the only US state where prostitution is legally permitted in some form. Prostitution is legal in ten of Nevada's seventeen counties, although only six allow it in every municipality. Six counties have at least one active brothel, which mainly operate in isolated, rural areas.

10. The Double Jeopardy Clause in the Fifth Amendment to the US Constitution prohibits anyone from being prosecuted twice for substantially the same crime.

11. The Torah (and later understood by the Talmud) specifies capital punishment by

the financial penalty is waived in the face of the possibility of capital punishment.[12] For example, were one to ritually slaughter a stolen ox (an act that carries a five-fold financial penalty) on the Sabbath (an act which, if done knowingly and with forewarnings of the consequences, subjects one to death by stoning), the individual is not assessed the financial penalty whether or not he is actually executed. Hence, no "double jeopardy."

The Talmud in Bava Kama[13] applies this principle to one who hires his mother as a prostitute (admittedly a disturbing but fascinating theoretical construct). While acknowledging that hiring a prostitute is a sinful activity, the Talmud rules that, if the couple engaged in sexual activities, the man must pay the woman for her services. We see from this that Judaism enforces legal obligations (payment to the prostitute) even in the face of morally objectionable activities (engaging in sexual activities with a prostitute). When would the women be barred from demanding her payment? If she were the mother of her "client." All financially liability here is waived not because sleeping with one's mother is violates Torah law (and is therefore illegal). It is waived solely in the face of a more severe consequence (capital punishment).

Under American law, contracting sexual services automatically voids the contract, not because prostitution is immoral, but because it is illegal. In Jewish law, the Talmudic sages require payment, notwithstanding their disgust over such an immoral and sinful act. It is only Judaism's unique understanding of "double jeopardy" that results in a void contract (to use American legal parlance).

Let us now examine some specific case studies that further underscore the complicated interplay of morality and legality in these two legal systems.

---

the "Four Executions of the Court"—stoning, burning, decapitation, and strangulation—for the most severe transgressions, among them murder, idol worship. and desecrating the Sabbath, as well as several seemingly less serious ones, like serially disobeying one's parents. Corporal punishment, that is lashes, is also considered a form of capital punishment in Jewish law and is applicable for intentional transgressions of any negative commandment that does not incur the death penalty.

12. In such cases, there is never a double penalty, that is, financial and capital.
13. Talmud Bavli Bava Kamma 70b.

Case Studies

ABORTION

Of all the case studies we might consider, none better exemplifies the dichotomy between morality and legality than the issues surrounding abortion rights. Even the names used by people engaged in the debate to differentiate themselves reflect this.

On one side, we have those who advocate for a women's right to choose. Pro-choice activists do not frame their arguments in terms of morality (even though some may have certain moral misgivings). They prefer to focus on the rights of women, which include the right to end a pregnancy, the right to carry out a wanted pregnancy, and the right to raise a child in a safe, healthy, and just society.[14] And so long as *Roe v. Wade*[15] was the law of the land, they also spoke of women's legal rights, especially the right to privacy implied in the Forteenth Amendment.

The other side refers to themselves as pro-life.[16] As the name suggests, pro-lifers are opposed to abortion, and their opposition often centers on a moral argument, namely, that abortion is murder.[17]

Before comparing and contrasting the approaches of secular and Jewish law to this emotionally charged topic, I would like to delve a bit deeper into the question of whether abortion ought to be viewed as murder.

Let's start with the American law perspective.

In colonial America and the early days of the republic, there were no abortion laws at all. Church officials frowned on the practice, but they treated it as evidence of illicit or premarital sex—not as murder. Some localities, however, did prosecute cases involving abortions. In 1740s Connecticut, for example, prosecutors tried both a doctor and a Connecticut man for a misdemeanor in connection with the death of Sarah Grosvenor, who had died after a botched abortion. Importantly, the case centered around the men's role in the woman's death, not abortion per se, and such prosecutions were rare.[18]

---

14. Segers, "The Language of Abortion Is Going Through a Seismic Overhaul."

15. *Roe v. Wade,* 410 U.S. 113 (1973).

16. In her *New Republic* article, Segers notes that advocates and politicians have recently begun to turn away from the "pro-choice" and "pro-life" labels.

17. See, for example, Potter, "Five Reasons Abortion is Murder."

18. How U.S. abortion laws went from nonexistent to acrimonious. Blakemore, "How US Abortion Laws Went from Nonexistent to Acrimonious."

Before 1840, abortion was a widespread, largely stigma-free experience for American women.[19] During that period, the American legal system used the quickening doctrine from British common law to decide the legality of abortion. Quickening occurred when the pregnant woman could feel the fetus move, typically between the fourth and sixth month of pregnancy. This was the only sure way to confirm pregnancy. Prior to this time, any fetus was considered only a potential life. Women most often used herbal concoctions they had learned from other women, healers, or physicians to cure their "obstructed menses" before quickening. Post-quickening abortion was a crime, but only a misdemeanor. Some historians have suggested that laws against post-quickening abortions were primarily intended to protect the health of the pregnant woman—not fetal life—as it was much more common for women to die during abortions that used instruments rather than herbal abortifacients. Whatever the rationale, few abortions were prosecuted before the mid-nineteenth century because quickening was so difficult to prove. Only women themselves could testify to fetal movement.

So what changed? And when?

Starting in the mid-nineteenth century, this system of legal but quiet abortions fell apart. The first "right-to-life" movement was actually led by physicians who were anxious about their professional status. Before then, physicians had been largely unregulated, without the institutional or cultural authority to corner the market on healing. In the early nineteenth century, a variety of other healers competed with physicians for business, especially the business of women's reproductive healthcare. In response to this competition, many physicians began to look for scientific medicine that they believed would benefit their patients. Others sought governmental licensing and regulation in an effort to weed out the competition. Ultimately, anti-abortion laws pushed in state legislatures worked to increase physicians' stature and undermine their opponents.

This effort largely succeeded. Criminalization of abortion took off in the late 1860s, when states began passing laws banning the procedure. By 1880, abortion was outlawed in most states. This wave of criminalizing legislation was furthered by the Comstock laws—officially, the Comstock Act of 1873, sometimes referred to as Anthony Comstock's "chastity laws"—that criminalied the sending of "obscene, lewd, or lascivious" materials in

---

19. The brief history of abortions in the nineteenth century that follows is taken from Holland, "Abolishing Abortion: The History of the Pro-Life Movement in America."

the mail and any information that related to birth control, sex, and methods of terminating a pregnancy. This began a century-long effort to restrict women's access to safe abortions. Even contraceptives were labeled as "illicit" or "obscene."

By 1900, every state had a law forbidding abortion at any stage, whether through the use of drugs or procedures. Almost all the laws passed during this time included a therapeutic exception, whereby licensed physicians could provide abortions at their own discretion as long as the abortion preserved the life of the mother. While this loophole allowed many women to obtain abortions, it also made doctors the ultimate arbiters of the morality and legality of abortions. These laws also created a large black market for women who could not access or obtain abortions through medical channels.

At no point during this time period was abortion equated with murder. Indeed, there was no talk of life beginning at conception. This would not happen until evangelical Christians started to tout "the biblical view" that life begins at birth.[20] As late as 1968, *Christianity Today*, the nation's leading evangelical magazine, hosted a gathering of evangelical leaders from across the country for a symposium on human procreation. Led by theologian Carl F.H. Henry, participants produced a joint statement representing "the conservative or evangelical position within Protestantism." While affirming that developing life has some value throughout pregnancy, they were not comfortable assigning full personhood until the very end. "From the moment of birth," the consensus statement affirmed, "the infant is a human being with all the rights which Scripture accords to all human beings."[21]

In case the authors had left any confusion as to "when life begins," one of the symposium participants clarified in an accompanying issue of *Christianity Today*:

> God does not regard the fetus as a soul, no matter how far gestation has progressed. The Law plainly exacts: "If a man kills any human life he will be put to death" (Lev. 24:17). But according to Exodus 21:22–24, the destruction of the fetus is not a capital

---

20. Proponents of this idea cite Genesis 2:7 as proof that human personhood begins once the "breath of life" enters the body.

21. Dudley, "When The 'Biblical View' For Evangelicals Was That Life Begins At Birth."

offense... Clearly, then, in contrast to the mother, the fetus is not reckoned as a soul.[22]

A 1967 issue of the evangelical magazine *Christian Life* went even further, castigating Catholics for their non-biblical stance:

> The Bible definitely pinpoints a difference in the value of a fetus and an adult. Thus, the Bible would appear to disagree with the official Catholic view that the tiniest fetus is as important as an adult human being.[23]

For its part, the Southern Baptist Convention issued a 1971 statement advocating liberalization of abortion laws in a range of circumstances, including if the emotional health of the mother was at risk. Wayne Dehoney, a former president of the Southern Baptist Convention, later explained the reasoning: "Protestant theology generally takes Genesis 2:7 as a statement that the soul is formed at breath, not with conception."[24]

So, again, we must ask, what changed? And when?

In truth, there was little need for an anti-abortion movement between 1900 and 1965 because the state did its work. Police, courts, and lawmakers prosecuted abortionists and harassed women who procured the procedure. However, in the 1960s, some Americans began to demand change from states' laws driven in part by a larger cultural shift in Americans' ideas about reproduction and abortion. Towards the end of that decade, a nascent feminist movement began to argue that women could not be full citizens unless they could control reproduction. Together, these shifts helped push state legislatures to reform their abortion laws. Colorado was the first to amend its law in 1967, followed quickly by others, most famously California in 1967 and New York in 1970.

Such reforms gave rise to the notion of "abortion on demand," and this marked a turning point in the abortion battles. Between 1967 and 1969, the magazines *Christianity Today*, *Eternity*, and *Christian Life* published several articles on abortion, all of which presented a similar conclusion: it was wrong to use abortion as a means of birth control, because abortion constituted the taking of an actual or a potential life. Nonetheless, they

---

22. Dudley, "When The 'Biblical View' For Evangelicals Was That Life Begins At Birth."

23. Dudley, "When The 'Biblical View' For Evangelicals Was That Life Begins At Birth."

24. Dudley, "When The 'Biblical View' For Evangelicals Was That Life Begins At Birth."

agreed, abortion was probably acceptable in cases of rape or in instances when a pregnancy threatened the life or health of a mother. A *Christianity Today* editorial from 1969 summarized the dominant evangelical view at the time when it declared: "Surely we should resist the taking of innocent lives of unborn infants merely on demand or for convenience. There must be substantial medical and other grounds that are biblically licit. Otherwise, abortion becomes murder."[25]

This was but the beginning.

The removal of almost all legal restrictions on first and second-trimester abortions in New York in 1970 was particularly troubling to those who opposed abortion, since it quickly led to nearly 200,000 legal abortions per year in New York's hospitals. Two months after the enactment of New York's new abortion policy, *Christianity Today* published an editorial titled, "War on the Womb," which argued, for the first time, that human personhood probably began "at the very moment or very soon after the sperm and egg meet."[26]

And so the dye was cast. Battlelines were drawn. And the Supreme Court opted to weigh in.

In 1973, the US Supreme Court issued its famous and much contested ruling in *Roe v. Wade*.[27] The Court recognized that the decision whether to continue or end a pregnancy belongs to the individual, not the government. *Roe* held that the specific guarantee of "liberty" in the Fourteenth Amendment of the US Constitution, which protects individual privacy, includes the right to abortion prior to fetal viability. The Court defined fetal viability as the ability of a fetus to live outside the womb, which usually happens between twenty-four and twenty-eight weeks after conception. It held that after fetal viability, outright bans on abortion were permitted if they contained exceptions to preserve life and health. However, the government could not ban abortions for any reason prior to viability.

The Court went on to add one additional caveat, one that would lead to legal challenges to *Roe*: the government retained the power to regulate or restrict abortion access depending on the stage of pregnancy. Nevertheless, the Court held that such infringements on a woman's right to an abortion should be narrowly tailored to serve a compelling government

---

25. Williams, "The Partisan Trajectory of the American Pro-Life Movement," 461.
26. Williams, "The Partisan Trajectory of the American Pro-Life Movement," 462.
27. *Roe v. Wade*, 410 U.S. 113 (1973).

interest.[28] Applying a trimester framework, *Roe* permitted more regulation of abortion as pregnancy advanced, but only when that regulation was evidence-based and consistent with how other similar medical procedures were treated.[29]

Post-*Roe*, questions regarding the power to regulate or restrict abortion access came up time and time again, most notably in these Supreme Court cases:

- In *Planned Parenthood v. Danforth* (1976), the justices blocked a law requiring spousal consent for abortion.
- *Maher v. Roe* (1979) permitted states to exclude abortion services from Medicaid coverage.
- *Colautti v. Franklin* (1979) struck down an unconstitutionally vague Pennsylvania law that required physicians to try to save the life of a fetus that might have been viable.
- In *Harris v. McRae* (1980), the Court upheld the Hyde Amendment, a federal law that proscribed federal funding for abortions except when necessary to preserve life or as a result of rape or incest.
- In *L. v. Matheson* (1981), the Court upheld a law requiring parental notification when the patient is a minor living with parents.
- In *City of Akron v. Akron Center for Reproductive Health* (1983), the justices invalidated a wide range of limitations on abortion, such as a waiting period, parental consent without judicial bypass, and a ban on abortions outside of hospitals after the first trimester.
- *Thornburgh v. American College of Obstetricians and Gynecologists* (1986) struck down a law that required informed consent to include information about fetal development and alternatives to abortion.
- In *Webster v. Reproductive Health Services* (1989), Justice Rehnquist upheld rules requiring doctors to test for viability after 20 weeks and blocking state funding and state employee participation in abortion services.

---

28. As defined by the Supreme Court, a government interest is compelling if it is essential or necessary rather than a matter of choice, preference, or discretion. *Palmore v. Sidoti*, 466 U.S. 429 (1984).

29. *Roe v. Wade*, 410 U.S. 113 (1973).

Case Studies

- *Rust v. Sullivan* (1991) upheld a ban on certain federal funds being used for abortion referrals or counseling.
- *Hill v. Colorado* (2000) upheld a law limiting protest and leafletting close to an abortion clinic.
- In *Gonzales v. Carhart* (2007), a slightly changed Court upheld a federal ban on the dilation and extraction procedure.

What is clear is that *Roe* did not settle the abortion debate, despite its holding that the right to privacy implied in the Fourteenth Amendment protected abortion as a fundamental right. Both sides spent decades fighting over the power of individual states to regulate or restrict abortion access. In the end, the anti-abortionists prevailed, and in June 2022, the Court overturned *Roe*, ruling there is no federal constitutional right to abortion. The ruling in *Dobbs v. Jackson Women's Health Organization*[30] abandoned nearly fifty years of precedent and marked the first time in history that the Supreme Court took away from America citizens what it had previously held to be a fundamental right.

Rather than clarifying or settling matters, the *Dobbs* decision made matters even murkier. The Court completely dodged the question of when does life begin, which seems to me to be the key question to resolve.[31] How so? If life begins at birth, the fetus has the potential of life, and it may be sinful to terminate that potential, but abortion cannot be murder. This is the view of Judaism and most Protestant denominations. If life begins at conception, as the Catholics maintain, then abortion is murder and should never be permitted, even in cases of rape and incest.[32] This is a question science cannot answer. Yet, by allowing states to pass and enforce complete abortion bans, *Dobbs* seems to have embraced the Catholic approach.[33]

30. *Dobbs v. Jackson Women's Health Organization*, 597 U.S. 215 (2022).

31. "The court said that when life begins is up to whoever is running your state—whether they are wrong or not, or you agree with them or not," said Mary Ziegler, a law professor at the University of California-Davis who has written several books on the history of abortion. Varney, "When Does Life Begin? As State Laws Define It, Science, Politics, and Religion Clash."

32. What to do when the mother's life is endangered is also a matter of debate. If only one can be saved, unborn child or mother, Catholics would opt to save the child, who must be baptized to avoid eternal damnation. Jews and Protestants would save the mother instead of the unborn child.

33. Certain religious groups—particularly Jewish groups—have argued that they have a right to abortion care. In Generation to Generation v. Florida, No. 2022 CA 980 (Fla. Cir. Ct. August 9, 2022), a religious rights group argued that Florida's abortion ban (HB

This is not hyperbole. It's fact. Since the Court issued its *Dobbs* decision, red states across much of the South and portions of the Midwest have adopted language drafted by elected officials that is informed by conservative Christian doctrine, often with little scientific underpinning.[34]

A handful of Republican-led states, including Arkansas, Kentucky, Missouri, and Oklahoma, have passed laws declaring that life begins at fertilization, a contention that opens the door to a host of pregnancy-related litigation. There seems to be no limit as to how far states will run with this notion, as illustrated by a February 2024 opinion issued by the Alabama Supreme Court. In it, the Court ruled that frozen embryos are children under state law and subject to legislation dealing with the wrongful death of a minor, stating that it "applies to all unborn children, regardless of their location."[35]

In Kentucky, the law outlawing abortion uses morally explosive terms to define pregnancy as "the human female reproductive condition of having a living unborn human being within her body throughout the entire embryonic and fetal stages of the unborn child from fertilization to full gestation and childbirth."

All this reenforces the idea we have previously put forward, namely, that the American legal system is not well equipped to deal with questions

---

5) constituted a violation of the Florida State Constitution: "In Jewish law, abortion is required if necessary to protect the health, mental or physical well-being of the woman, or for many other reasons not permitted under the Act. As such, the Act prohibits Jewish women from practicing their faith free of government intrusion and thus violates their privacy rights and religious freedom." Similar cases have arisen in Indiana and Texas. Absent constitutional protection of abortion rights, the Christian religious majorities in many states may unjustly impose their moral and ethical code on other groups, implying an unconstitutional religious hierarchy. Cipriano, "The First Amendment and the Abortion Rights Debate."

34. This conclusion and the examples that follow can be found in Varney, "When Does Life Begin? As State Laws Define It, Science, Politics, and Religion Clash."

35. Choi, "Alabama Supreme Court Rules Frozen Embryos are 'Children.'" Lest anyone doubt the extent to which morality drives the ongoing debates in America about abortion and reproductive rights, just read the concurring opinion penned by Chief Justice Tom Parker in this case. In discussing the phrase "the sanctity of unborn life" in the Alabama Constitution, Parker writes: "Even before birth, all human beings bear the image of God, and their lives cannot be destroyed without effacing his glory." He continues: "We believe that each human being, from the moment of conception, is made in the image of God, created by Him to reflect His likeness. It is as if the People of Alabama took what was spoken of the prophet Jeremiah and applied it to every unborn person in this state: 'Before I formed you in the womb I knew you, Before you were born I sanctified you.' Jeremiah 1:5 (NKJV 1982)."

of morality. It is thus not surprising that the post-*Dobbs* legal environment is messy, because at its core, one's view on abortion is driven by the individual's morals. Aborting a fetus that one considers to be a fully human being is morally repugnant. Aborting a fetus that one considers to simply be part of a woman's body is a relatively routine medical procedure.[36] It is just not reasonable to expect the Supreme Court (or any court for that matter) to equitably or logically split the difference between these very different moral underpinnings.

Jewish law also recognizes the moral component to this debate. In Jewish law, abortion on demand is sinful, as was made abundantly clear by the Union of Orthodox Jewish Congregations of America[37] in a statement released post-*Dobbs*:

> We cannot support absolute bans on abortion—at any time point in a pregnancy—that would not allow access to abortion in lifesaving situations. Similarly, we cannot support legislation that permits "abortion on demand"—at any time point in a pregnancy—and does not confine abortion to situations in which medical (including mental health) professionals affirm that carrying the pregnancy to term poses real risk to the life of the mother. . . Abortion on demand—the "right to choose" (as well as the "right to die")—are completely at odds with our religious and halachic values.[38]

Sinful? Yes. Murder? Certainly not, and for a simple reason. As the Talmud states in numerous places, *ubar yerekh imo*, that is, the fetus is "part of its mother."[39] In other places, the Talmud refers to the fetus as "one of her limbs."[40] Both references involve questions of ownership, such as in the case of an embryo found in a purchased animal. More telling are the laws of ritual impurity in which an embryo is deemed to be one with its

---

36. This is, admittedly, a bit simplistic, as there is research showing that abortion is consistently associated with elevated rates of mental illness compared to women without a history of abortion and that the abortion experience directly contributes to mental health problems for at least some women. Reardon, "The Abortion and Mental Health Controversy: A Comprehensive Literature Review of Common Ground Agreements, Disagreements, Actionable Recommendations, and Research Opportunities."
37. The Orthodox Union, of the OU as it is commonly referred to, is one of the largest Orthodox Jewish organizations in the United States.
38. Eisenberg, "Abortion in Jewish Law."
39. Talmud Bavli Hulin 58a and other places.
40. Talmud Bavli Gittin 23b.

mother.⁴¹ And then there are the laws of conversion involving a pregnant woman. Her unborn child is automatically included in her conversation and requires no further ceremony.⁴²

The idea that abortion is not murder is further supported by the fact that the Torah merely requires a monetary payment for causing a miscarriage. This is interpreted by many rabbinical scholars to indicate that abortion is not a capital crime.⁴³

The Talmudic discussions cited above do not touch upon the morality of terminating a pregnancy. Rather, they merely define the legal status of the fetus. In Jewish law, as was the case in ancient Roman law, the fetus has no "juridical personality" of its own.⁴⁴ This, of course, stands in sharp contrast with states such as Georgia that, post-*Dobbs*, have adopted measures equating life with the point at which an embryo's nascent cardiac activity can be detected by an ultrasound, at around six weeks of gestation. Many such laws mischaracterize the flickering electrical impulses detectible at that stage as a heartbeat, including in Georgia, whose Department of Revenue recently announced that "any unborn child with a detectable human heartbeat" can be claimed as a dependent.⁴⁵

While a fetus has no "juridical personality" of its own, Jewish law does not leave it unprotected. A fetus is treated in most circumstances like any other "person" in the sense that one may not deliberately harm it.⁴⁶ Jewish law also holds accountable one who purposefully causes a woman to miscarry, and sanctions are even placed upon one who strikes a pregnant woman causing an unintentional miscarriage.⁴⁷

This leaves us to ask, under what circumstances, if any, does Jewish law sanction abortion? The basic starting point is this. There is universal agreement in the sources that the fetus will become a full-fledged human being. Hence, there must be very compelling reasons to allow it, and the Mishnah provides one:

---

41. Talmud Bavli Nazir 51a.
42. Talmud Bavli Yevamot 78a.
43. Rashi and *Yad Ramah* to Talmud Bavli Sanhedrin 57b. See also Rabbi Yehuda, *Be'er Hetiv*, Choshen Mishpat 425:2.
44. Feldman, *Marital Relations*, 254.
45. Varney, "When Does Life Begin? As State Laws Define It, Science, Politics, and Religion Clash.
46. *Igros Moshe*, Choshen Mishpat II: 69B.
47. *Shulchan Aruch*, Choshen Mishpat, 423:1.

Case Studies

> If a woman is having trouble giving birth, they cut up the child in her womb and brings it forth limb by limb, because her life comes before the life of [the child].[48]

Importantly, this Mishnah concludes with a crucial caveat, one that provides the basis of Judaism's view that life only begins with the birth of the child:

> But if the greater part has come out, one may not touch it, for one may not set aside one person's life for that of another.

This Mishnah sets forth an important general rule: abortion is permitted only if there is a direct threat to the life of the mother by carrying the fetus to term or through the act of childbirth. In such a circumstance, the baby is considered tantamount to a *rodef*, a pursuer after the mother with the intent to kill her.[49]

This is an excellent rule of thumb, but it harkens back to our discussion of foundational texts and their binding nature. Just as the Torah's mandate "You shall not murder" does not provide us with sufficient legal guidance to adjudicate certain capital cases, so, too, with this ruling of the Mishnah as explained by the commentators. How do we define "the intent to kill her?"[50]

---

48. Mishnah Oholot 7:6. Maimonides accepts this as normative Jewish law. *Mishneh Torah*, Hilkhot Rotzeah Ush'mirat Nefesh 1:9.

49. Maimonides, *Mishneh Torah*, Laws of Murder 1:9; Talmud Bavli Sanhedrin 72B. Despite the classification of the fetus as a pursuer, once the baby's head or most of its body has been delivered, the baby's life is considered equal to that of the mother, and we may not choose one life over another, because it is considered as though they are both pursuing each other. See Eisenberg, "Abortion in Jewish Law."

50. The discussion that follows is based on Orthodox Judaism's approaches to abortion. The Conservative movement is somewhat more lenient in such cases, explicitly understanding threats to a mother's life as extending to psychological threats to her mental well-being. In 1983, the Conservative movement's rabbinical authorities permitted abortion only "if a continuation of pregnancy might cause the mother severe physical or psychological harm, or when the fetus is judged by competent medical opinion as severely defective." The Reform movement has historically taken a similar approach. In 1958, the movement's rabbinate determined that abortion is permitted for sake of the mother's mental well-being if there is "strong preponderance of medical opinion that the child will be born imperfect physically, and even mentally." In 1985, the psychological justification was explicitly extended to cases of rape and incest, while emphasizing opposition to abortion for "trivial reasons" or "on demand." In published responsa, the movement has rejected abortion in cases where the birth might pose hardships for other family members. At the same time, both the Reform and Conservative rabbinates have been vocal in support of keeping abortion legal and accessible. My Jewish Learning,

First, we must note that the reason the life of the fetus is subordinate to the mother is because the fetus is the cause of the mother's life-threatening condition. Whether this is due to direct consequences of the pregnancy (e.g., due to toxemia, placenta previa, or breach position) or indirect consequences (e.g., exacerbation of underlying diabetes, kidney disease, or hypertension), the threat to the mother is real, and the pregnancy may be terminated.[51]

Second, let us also note that life-threatening conditions are not limited in Jewish law to the physical. They extend to the mental as well, and precedent for equating mental health with physical health dates to the late-seventeenth-century. The degree of mental illness that must be present to justify termination of a pregnancy has been widely debated by rabbinic scholars. While there is no clear consensus of opinion regarding the exact criteria for permitting abortion in such instances, some examples do stand out.

Insanity alone is not deemed to be life-threatening, as the insane have the same instinct for self-preservation as the sane. It thus does not justify allowing an abortion. However, insanity accompanied with suicidal tendencies or attacks of hysteria is seen as a matter of life-and-death, as the inflicted individual can do physical harm to self or to others. Moreover, suicidal tendencies brought on by the pregnancy itself are a threat to the woman and as such constitute adequate grounds for permitting an abortion.[52]

Another form of mental anguish discussed in the sources is that which accompanies a pregnancy brought about by an adulterous relationship. A prominent seventeenth century *posek* saw no clear prohibition against an abortion in such circumstances, but nevertheless refused to sanction the procedure out of a concern that it would "open the door to immorality."[53] Others, such as Rabbi Jacob Emden (eighteenth century) and Chief Rabbi Ben Zion Uziel (twentieth century), disagreed. Citing the "great pain"

"Abortion and Judaism."

51. Eisenberg, "Abortion in Jewish Law." It goes without saying that a fetus may not be aborted to save the life of any other person whose life is not directly threatened by the fetus, such as use of fetal organs for transplant.

52. Feldman, *Marital Relations*, 285. This would seem to support abortion in cases of rape and incest.

53. Feldman, *Marital Relations*, 288.

suffered by remorseful woman, they found room to permit the procedure when disgrace is involved.[54]

Third, Jewish law does not assign relative values to different lives. Therefore, most major *poskim* forbid abortion in cases of abnormalities or deformities found in a fetus. Rabbi Eliezar Yehuda Waldenberg is a notable exception. Rabbi Waldenberg allows first trimester abortion of a fetus that would be born with a deformity that would cause it to suffer, and termination of a fetus with a lethal fetal defect such as Tay Sachs up to the seventh month of gestation.[55] The rabbinic experts also discuss the permissibility of abortion for mothers with German measles and babies with prenatal confirmed Down syndrome.[56]

A fascinating corollary addresses the danger a pregnancy poses to the health of an existing child. The case involved a nursing woman whose milk was affected by her pregnancy and whose infant could not substitute formula feeding, as attested to by physicians. The rabbinic authorities who ruled on the matter held that an abortion would be justified to protect the health of her child.[57]

In the end, what do we take away from all this?

In the case of abortion, American law has tried to resolve questions like "when does life begin?". Even though these types of questions are best left to theologians and philosophers, not lawyers (or even scientists). Layered upon this is its penchant for emphasizing legality over morality, which left it searching in vain for a single legal solution to an incredibly complex issue, be it the twenty-four-week standard set by *Roe* or the sixteen-week national standard many politicians discussed during the 2024 election cycle or even the fetal heartbeat standard adopted by several states post-*Dobbs*. The result? Each day, countless woman across American are denied necessary medical treatments out of fears that the procedures might violate their state's rigid anti-abortion laws, denials that put their health and sometimes their lives at risk.[58]

In contrast, Jewish law, because of its theological underpinnings, is able to derive definitively that life begins with the birth of the child, not

---

54. Feldman, *Marital Relations*, 288–289. See also Abraham, *Nishmat Avraham*, Choshen Mishpat, 425, 293.

55. *Tzitz Eliezer*, Volume 13:102.

56. Eisenberg, "Abortion in Jewish Law."

57. Feldman, *Marital Relations*, 287.

58. El-Bawab, Scott, Ng, and Nunes, "Delayed and Denied."

before. This does not lead it to sanction abortion on demand, as the OU made quite clear in its post-*Dobbs* statement, nor does it grant a fetus legal status as a human being. With its emphasis on doing "what is good and right in the sight of God,"[59] Jewish law permits abortions when the physical or at times mental wellbeing of the mother is at risk. This produces not a single, "one size fits all" approach, but diverse outcomes that can and do differ on a case-by-case basis.

LGBTQ RIGHTS

LGBTQ rights are a logical bookend in two ways to our discussion of abortion. First, whereas abortion showcases the many problems that arise when America law veers into issues of morality, LGBTQ rights represent the law's effort to stop applying external moral standards to people's personal lives.[60] Second, when it comes to abortion, Jewish law largely avoids a single solution approach. It recognizes that abortion questions (other than those involving abortion on demand) should be dealt with on a case-by-case basis. Nevertheless, Jewish law's answer to most LGBTQ questions can be boiled down to a single answer (no), whereas American law continues to carve out new rights for the LGBTQ community.

The approach of both legal systems to LBGTQ rights was initially driven by the Bible's clear condemnation of same-sex relations: "Do not lie with a male as one lies with a woman; it is an abhorrence (תּוֹעֵבָה)."[61] Despite the seeming unambiguity of the English translations of תּוֹעֵבָה, the true meaning of this word is not so clear. Common translations such as abhorrence or abomination are passion-wrought, pejorative terms. Consider this single example as demonstrating the point. ArtScroll's *The Chumash: The Stone Edition*, which is used by hundreds of Orthodox congregations across America, offers this explanation of our verse:

> The chapter of immorality ends with two forms of sexual perversion: homosexuality and bestiality. The harshness with which the Torah describes

---

59. Deuteronomy 6:18.

60. Although the ongoing brouhaha at the state level regarding transgender rights runs counter to this.

61. Leviticus 18:22. It is important to note that the verse refers specifically to male-on-male penetrative sex, that is, anal intercourse

them testifies to the repugnance in which God holds those who engage in these unnatural practices (emphasis added).[62]

Is this a fair reading of the verse? Some believe so. However, the term תּוֹעֵבָה does not necessarily convey the angst and passion of the English words abhorrence and abomination.[63] For instance, some argue that תּוֹעֵבָה is used in this and other sexual contexts precisely because these commandments are legislated regarding behaviors that people's instincts incline them towards. The Bible thus uses very strong language to condemn these behaviors as a lever to persuade individuals to suppress their instincts.

Regardless of how one translates the biblical term תּוֹעֵבָה, American society was generally shaped for decades by a restrictive and harsh understanding of the word, and as a result, so was American law. Thus, the legal protections that are today afforded to members of the LGBTQ community took a long and arduous path.

SAME-SEX RELATIONS IN AMERICAN LAW

In 1924, Henry Gerber, a German immigrant, founded the Society for Human Rights in Chicago, the first documented gay rights organization in the United States. Gerber's small group published a few issues of its newsletter "Friendship and Freedom," which was the country's first gay-interest newsletter. Police raids caused the group to disband in 1925, but ninety years later, the US government designated Gerber's Chicago house a National Historic Landmark.[64]

Gerber's efforts were a bit of an outlier. In truth, there were few attempts to create advocacy groups supporting gay and lesbian relationships until after World War II. The war may have brought very diverse demographic groups together on the front lines, Blacks and Whites, gays and straights, but little changed when these individuals returned home. Indeed, the 1950s were perilous times for LBGTQ individuals. Many cities formed "vice squads" that actively sought to track down "homosexuals,"[65] although the police often labeled the people they arrested "sexual perverts."

62. *The Chumash*, 653.
63. Feder, "Terms of Taboo."
64. History.com Editors, "Gay Rights."
65. This term was popularized by pioneering German psychiatrist Richard von Krafft-Ebing. In the US, professionals often used the term "invert." "Government Persecution of the LGBTQ Community is Widespread."

Between the Laws of God and Man

The government's preferred term was "deviant," which came with legal consequences for anyone seeking a career in public service or the military.

Not surprisingly, few members of the LGBTQ community dared to openly express themselves in these years. However, there were a number of courageous activists working to secure LGBTQ rights. Take Harry Hay as an example. In 1950, he founded the Mattachine Foundation, one of the nation's first gay rights group, which sought to improve the lives of gay men through discussion groups and related activities. Although it started off small, the foundation expanded after founding member Dale Jennings was arrested in 1952 for solicitation and then later set free due to a deadlocked jury. At the end of the year, Jennings formed another organization called One, Inc., which welcomed women and published *ONE*, the country's first gay rights magazine.[66] Then, in 1955, four lesbian couples in San Francisco founded an organization called the Daughters of Bilitis, which soon began publishing a newsletter called *The Ladder*, the first lesbian publication of any kind.

Despite such achievements, the 1950s were replete with setbacks for the fledgling movement. In 1952, the American Psychiatric Association listed homosexuality as a form of mental disorder. (It was only in 1973 that the American Psychiatric Association removed homosexuality as an "illness" classification in its diagnostic manual.) In 1953, President Dwight D. Eisenhower signed an executive order that banned gay people—or, more specifically, people guilty of "sexual perversion"—from federal jobs. This ban would remain in effect for some twenty years.

Worst still was the "Lavender Scare."

Most Americans are familiar with Senator Joseph McCarthy and his push in the 1950s to purge suspected communists from government service and in Hollywood as well. This was part of his larger project to rid America of its "undesirable elements," elements, which included LBGTQ individuals. His targeting of gay men came to be known as the "Lavendar Scare." On two occasions, McCarthy specifically spoke on the Senate floor about cases concerning homosexuality. "Case 14" was, according to McCarthy, a known homosexual who had been ousted by the State Department but then rehired. In his discussion of that man and of "Case 62," McCarthy directly linked homosexuality and communism. A top intelligence official

---

66. Jennings was ousted from *One*, Inc. in 1953 in part for being a communist—he and Harry Hay were also kicked out of the Mattachine Foundation for their communism—but the magazine continued. History.com Editors, "Gay Rights."

had reportedly told him that "practically every active Communist is twisted mentally or physically in some way." McCarthy implied that the men in these two cases were susceptible to communist recruitment because as homosexuals they had what he called "peculiar mental twists." Shortly after these pronouncements, Deputy Undersecretary of State John Peurifoy, testifying before a subcommittee of the Senate Committee on Appropriations, revealed that the State Department had ousted ninety-one homosexual employees as security risks.[67]

The 1960s saw the beginnings of real breakthroughs in the fight for LGBTQ rights, as activists who were inspired by Civil Rights movement began to employ its tactics and strategies. Some were motivated by Thurgood Marshall, who was the leading architect of a strategy that sought to end ended state-sponsored segregation via legal challenges and legislative actions.[68] A early success came in 1961, when Illinois became the first state to do away with its anti-sodomy laws, effectively decriminalizing homosexuality. Others opted to follow the path of Dr. Martin Luther King Jr., who consistently adhered to nonviolent campaigns in the pursuit of equal rights for African Americans.[69] In the wake of these efforts, the first gay rights demonstrations took place in Philadelphia and Washington, DC, led by longtime activists Frank Kameny and Barbara Gittings.

Not all the milestones of the 1960s were peaceful, and virtually all historians agree that the turning point for gay liberation was marked by violence. On June 28, 1969, patrons of the popular Stonewall Inn in New York's Greenwich Village fought back against ongoing police raids of their neighborhood bar. The subsequent disturbances and rioting lasted six days.[70] Stonewall is still considered a watershed moment of the gay rights movement and has been commemorated since the 1970s with "gay pride marches" held every June across the United States.

After Stonewall, a more radical political consciousness developed in the LGBTQ community. Many new groups were formed, including the

---

67. Adkins, "'These People Are Frightened to Death.'"
68. "Thurgood Marshall."
69. King made this clear in his "Letter from a Birmingham Jail," in which he wrote: "In any nonviolent campaign there are four basic steps: (1) collection of the facts to determine whether injustices are alive; (2) negotiation; (3) self-purification; and (4) direct action. . . . Nonviolent direct action seeks to create such a crisis and establish such creative tension that a community that has constantly refused to negotiate is forced to confront the issue." King Jr., "Letter from a Birmingham Jail."
70. Downs, "The Gay Liberation Movement."

Gay Liberation Front and Radicalesbians,[71] whose members rejected these strategies and called for a more militant response to homophobia. These groups were interested not just in gaining rights but also in challenging systems of power like capitalism, which they believed oppressed them. They viewed Stonewall as an opportunity to revolutionize society and to rethink the meaning of sexuality. They drew on theories advanced by early twentieth-century sexologist Magnus Hirschfield and others to conceptualize their relationships and identities.[72]

For the LGBTQ community, the 1980s is remembered as a tragic era because of the AIDS crisis.[73] Yet, the decade was also marked by the galvanizing of the LGBTQ community brought about by the Supreme Court's decision in *Bowers v. Hardwick*.[74]

Bowers was not the first case to touch upon issues involving the LGBTQ community. Beginning in the 1950s, cases invoked the First Amendment to successfully challenge post office seizures of lesbian and gay publications as allegedly obscene, including one victorious case that made it all the way to the Supreme Court in 1958.[75] Successful freedom of speech cases also struck down bans on gay student groups at public colleges and universities, refusals to issue parade permits for gay rights demonstrations, denials of nonprofit status to gay rights organizations, and exclusions of lesbian and gay groups from public fora. These, and judicial limits that began to be placed on government efforts to close gay bars, were essential to making it possible in the years before the internet for LGBTQ people to learn about and meet one another and to organize for political and social change.[76]

---

71. Frustrated with the male leadership of most gay liberation groups, lesbians influenced by the feminist movement of the 1970s formed their own collectives, record labels, music festivals, newspapers, bookstores, and publishing houses, and called for lesbian rights in mainstream feminist groups like the National Organization for Women.

72. Downs, "The Gay Liberation Movement."

73. In June 1981, the CDC published a report on five previously healthy young gay men diagnosed with KS/OI. This was the first recognized sign of what would become known as "AIDS," a term officially coined in September 1982 by the CDC. AIDS incidence increased rapidly through the 1980s, peaked in the early 1990s, and then declined. As of December 31, 2000, 774,467 Americans had been reported with AIDS, resulting in the death of 448,060 individuals. "HIV and AIDS—United States, 1981–2000."

74. *Bowers v. Hardwick*, 478 U.S. 186 (1986).

75. *One, Inc. v. Olesen*, 355 U.S. 371 (1958) was the first US Supreme Court ruling to deal with homosexuality and the first to address free speech rights with respect to homosexuality.

76. Davidson, "A Brief History of the Path to Securing LGBTQ Rights."

Case Studies

By 1986, half the states had eliminated these laws either by legislative action or, in a few states, by lawsuits challenging them as violating state or federal constitutional protections. Nevertheless, in that same year, the Supreme Court issued its *Bowers* ruling and determined that the US Constitution did not prohibit states from criminalizing oral and anal sex between same-sex couples. The Court held that moral condemnation of homosexuality justified such laws, and, as we have demonstrated, mixing law and morality rarely leads to lasting or positive outcomes in the American judicial system.

The *Bowers* decision was widely derided. It also motivated the LGBTQ community to form numerous new organizations to fight for legal reforms. Public interest legal groups turned to state constitutions im an effort to uncouple law and morality. The results included successful state lawsuits that eliminated the sodomy laws of Arkansas, Georgia, Kentucky, Maryland, Montana, and Tennessee. Ultimately, the Supreme Court itself acknowledged that its decision in *Bowers* was "not correct when it was decided" and overturned that precedent.[77]

In American law, the Supreme Court is supposed to have the final word. Yet its attempt in this instance to distance morality and the law was not universally accepted. Continuing debates about the legal status of same-sex marriage demonstrates this.

In 1996, Congress passed the Defense of Marriage Act (DOMA). This legislation defined marriage at the federal level as the union of one man to one woman and allowed states to refuse to recognize same-sex marriages granted under the laws of other states. The Congress, in the House Judiciary Committee Report that accompanied the passage of DOMA, laid out its clear intent in enacting the law:

> There are, then, significant practical reasons why government affords preferential status to the institution of heterosexual marriage. These reasons—procreation and child-rearing—are in accord with nature and hence have a moral component. But they are not—or at least are not necessarily—moral or religious in nature. For many Americans, there is to this issue of marriage an overtly moral or religious aspect that cannot be divorced from the practicalities. It is true, of course, that the civil act of marriage is separate from the

---

77. In what was clearly a turning point for LGBTQ rights, the Court held that gay people were "entitled to respect for their private lives" and that the government "cannot demean their existence or control their destiny by making their private sexual conduct a crime." *Lawrence v. Texas*, 539 U.S. 558 (2003).

recognition and blessing of that act by a religious institution. But the fact that there are distinct religious and civil components of marriage does not mean that the two do not intersect. Civil laws that permit only heterosexual marriage reflect and honor a collective moral judgment about human sexuality. This judgment entails both moral disapproval of homosexuality, moral conviction that heterosexuality better comports with traditional (especially Judeo-Christian) morality.[78]

In the end, the Supreme Court in *United States v. Windsor*[79] ruled that DOMA was unconstitutional under the equal protection clause of the Fifth Amendment. In 2015, the Supreme Court took the next step and ruled in *Obergefell v. Hodges*[80] that same-sex couples in the United States, no matter where they live, have the same legal right to marry as different-sex couples.

SAME-SEX RELATIONS IN JEWISH LAW

When it comes to the issue of same-sex relations in Jewish law, there is no uncertainty, at least not in the Orthodox community. All agree that same-sex relations violate biblical law or rabbinic ordinances or, in certain cases, both. This is because Orthodox Judaism views the Torah as a foundational, binding, and closed text. The Reform and Conservative movements in America also see the Torah as foundational, but for these denominations, it is not binding or closed, especially with it comes to same-sex relations. Both denominations have thus resolved the issue by declaring that same-sex relations are no longer sinful.[81] That is not an option for Orthodox

---

78. US Congress, "Defense of Marriage Act."

79. *United States v. Windsor*, 570 U.S. 744 (2013).

80. *Obergefell v. Hodges*, 576 U.S. 644 (2015).

81. The Reform Movement's Central Conference of American Rabbis (CCAR) issued a resolution in March 2000 resolving that "the relationship of a Jewish, same-gender couple is worthy of affirmation through appropriate Jewish ritual and further resolve, that we recognize the diversity of opinions within our ranks on this issue." Similarly, the Committee on Jewish Law and Standards, which interprets religious law for the Conservative movement of Judaism, ruled in December 2006 that intimate relations between two men or two women are permitted within the context of a recognizable consecrated relationship. These rulings were based on each movement's respective understandings of the divine nature of the Bible. Reform Judaism contends that the Torah was written by humans. Rosenberg, "Can a reform Jew Believe the Torah is the Word of God?" The Conservative movement maintains that the Torah and Talmud, on which Jewish law is based, are human interpretations of the unchanging laws of God rather than the actual

Case Studies

Jewry, but neither is pretending that the issue does not exist or that it will somehow magically solve itself. Ignoring the pain and alienation of members of the Jewish community is neither just nor moral. How to balance this with the demands of Jewish law in this arena has yet to be determined, but it is worth discussing nonetheless.[82]

To be clear, discussions of LGBTQ issues in Orthodox circles are very complicated, in part due to the pejorative emotions typically associated with the Hebrew term תּוֹעֵבָה. Speaking dispassionately, there are people who claim to be or aspire to be affiliated with an Orthodox Jewish community who regularly violate Jewish dietary laws[83] or the laws of family purity or even the laws of Sabbath.[84] Yet, despite their repeated violations of Torah law, such individuals are welcomed in many Orthodox communities and are even sought after by synagogues who see themselves engaged in *kiruv*,

---

binding laws themselves. Hepler, "Conservative Judaism: Definition, History & Beliefs." Both movements therefore believe that the practices of Judaism are open to change with the rise of modernism, and both have dismissed the Bible's prohibition on homosexual activity as outdated and misinformed.

82. I believe that same-sex relations pose a theological conundrum that is beyond the scope of the book, but it is one that must nonetheless be noted. Sexual orientation has long been the subject of scientific study, and the reason why some individuals develop a gay sexual identity remains an open question. The American Psychological Association (APA) in 2010 took the position that a variety of factors impact a person's sexuality. The APA maintains that sexual orientation is not a choice that can be changed at will. Rather, sexual orientation is most likely the result of a complex interaction of environmental, cognitive, and biological factors [and] is shaped at an early age. Lamanna, Riedmann, and Stewart. *Marriages, Families, and Relationships*, 82. Others believe there is evidence that demonstrates the biological underpinnings of sexual orientation. See, for example, Ngun and Vilain, "The biological basis of human sexual orientation: is there a role for epigenetics?" If true, this begs the question of why God would create individuals with a biological inclination towards same-sex relations and then explicitly forbid such relations in the Torah. It seems so cruel to do so and flies in the face of Judaism's view of a merciful and benevolent God.

83. According to a 2013 Pew Research Center Study on American Jewish beliefs and practices, respondents who identified as Orthodox or Modern Orthodox were most likely to keep kosher homes, at rates of 98 percent and 83 percent respectively. In other words, as many as 17 percent of ritually observant Jews violate Jewish dietary laws. Pew Research Center, "A Portrait of Jewish Americans."

84. According to data released by the Pew Research Center in 2021, only four-in-ten US Jews say they often (20 percent) or sometimes (19 percent) mark Sabbath in a way that is meaningful to them. For some this might include traditional practices like resting, attending religious services, or lighting candles. For others, it might involve gathering with friends or doing community service. Pew Research Center. "Jewish American in 2020."

or outreach, activities. This stands in sharp contrast to LGBTQ individuals, who are often shunned by these very same communities because their lifestyles not only violate Torah law, but are also seen as an "abomination."

Many far wiser and more learned than I have noted the danger this represents to Jewish continuity.[85] They maintain that Orthodox communities can no longer avoid dealing with this issue. Continuing to do so risks alienating their supporters as well as younger members of their communities for whom the LGBTQ lifestyle is seen as a normal part of the world in which they live, learn, and work. It also has the potential to divide Jews at a time when they need to be united, more so perhaps than at any other time in decades.

We also see in this issue how modern times present significant challenges to Jewish law's mandate to balance the legal with the moral. A bit of background will help give this the context we need to fully grasp the many questions raised with regards to LGBTQ rights.

As is the case with many Talmudic discussions, the sages' consideration of sinful behavior involved theoretical categorizations. They compared and contrasted those who sinned in private out of desire (*mumar lete'avon*) with those who did so publicly and defiantly (*mumar le'hachis*). These prototypical sinners are like stick figure characters, representing absolutes and lacking in nuance. Not surprisingly, the sages' reactions to both also tended to be absolute and without nuance. Individuals driven to sin by desires they could not control and sometimes did not understand were seen by the sages as "remorseful sinners" and were thus deserving of empathy and sometimes even sympathy. However, ideological sinners, that is, those who were rebellious and took pride in their sins, received neither sympathy nor welcome from the sages.

The Talmud's theoretical categorization of sin is of far less useful on a practical level in today's real world. How are we to process and react to the behaviors of individuals who regularly and contentedly sins in private? Do we show them sympathy or shun them? This, of course, is the core question we wrestle with regarding the LBGTQ community.

There is precedent in Jewish law for not shunning them.

On what is the most solemn night on the Jewish calendar, Kol Nidre (the eve of Yom Kippur), those attending the prayer service make a somewhat startling declaration: "With the consent of the Almighty, and consent of this congregation, in a convocation of the heavenly court, and

---

85. Brander, "Finding a Home in our Midst."

a convocation of the lower court, we hereby grant permission to pray with transgressors."[86] Nowhere in this text are there definitions of sins. It merely affirms that all Jewish communities have sinners in their midst. There are those who cheat in business or cheat on their spouses. There are those who regularly violate Sabbath or never observe the family purity laws. And yes, there are those who engage in same-sex relations. All of them have one thing in common: a desire to be part of the Jewish community and take part in the Kol Nidre ritual. I believe that Rabbi Brander got it right when he wrote: "Singling out gay and lesbian Jews as less deserving of a place in the Jewish community reflects an imbalance in our values and therefore constitutes a form of societal discrimination."[87]

From a halachic perspective, there are many rulings that permit the participation of public Sabbath violators in the rituals of synagogue life.[88] The rabbinic mindset underlying such rulings was perhaps best summed up by Rabbi Yaakov Yisrael Kanievsky, the Steipler Rav. In essence, if people come to synagogue despite not being Sabbath observant, the community should not hesitate to include them, because this indicates that they feel an unbreakable connection to *yidishkeyt* (the Jewish way of life).[89] Today, many believe that a similar mindset ought to apply to those individuals involved in same-sex relations. In fact, Rabbi Eliezer Melamed made this point explicitly when he wrote that just as the Jewish community is comfortable counting those who are not Sabbath-observant in a *minyan* (the quorum required for a Jewish prayer service) and giving them ritual honors such as *aliyot* (being called up to the Torah), the same should be true of gay Jews, even if they are openly in a same-sex relationship.[90]

All this underscores an assertion made by Rabbi Brander and others when they said that making LBGTQ individuals feel welcome in Orthodox communities is a matter of public policy, not law.

---

86. My Jewish Learning. "Text of Kol Nidre."

87. Brander, "Finding a Home in our Midst," 8.

88. For example, Rabbi David Zvi Hofffman permitted non-Sabbath observant males to be counted as part of a *minyan*. Rabbi Moshe Feinstein allowed such individuals to receive *aliyot* to the Torah. Some synagogues even began offering additional, very early prayer services intended for those wished to pray on Sabbath mornings before going to work. Gurock, *Orthodox Jews in America*, 99–101, 160.

89. Brander, "Finding a Home in our Midst," 8.

90. Melamed, "Regarding LGBT—Education and Love."

Summary

When it comes to LBGTQ issues, the contrast here between Jewish law and American law is quite glaring. Jewish law is struggling with social acceptance of people who are engaged in activities still deemed sinful by Torah law. American law is working to unravel and remove legal barriers that were put into place to prohibit activities once deemed to be socially unacceptable (if not outright sinful) but that are now common and acceptable to most Americans.[91]

LGBTQ rights make for an enlightening case study. What we have here are two legal systems that are struggling to cope with changing societal norms. From the perspective of American law, this has meant changing, overturning, and rewriting laws in place for years and years. Why? Because same-sex relations, which were so frowned upon and condemned by society in previous generations, are now considered normal and acceptable. The challenge Jewish law faces is much more complicated. While it is true that general society is more accepting of same-sex relations, the biblical prohibition remains in place, at least in the Orthodox world. Modern rabbinic leaders are thus engaged in a delicate balancing act. How can they welcome individuals in same-sex relations into their communities while concurrently not condoning an activity prohibited by the Bible? Must they hate the sin, but love the sinner? This makes for a catchy phrase, but in reality, it does not easily lend itself to sound public policies.

ASSISTED SUICIDE

In our previous two cases studies, there seemed to be a disconnect between the will of the people and the direction undertaken by the judicial and political systems. The Supreme Court held in *Dobbs* that women do not have a constitutionally protected right to abortion and that the power to regulate any aspect of abortion not protected by federal law rests with individual states. Within six months of the *Dobbs* decision, a total of twenty-one states had banned abortion or restricted the procedure earlier in pregnancy than the twenty-four—week standard that had been set by *Roe*

---

91. According to Wikipedia, a September 2022 *Grinnell College National Poll* found that 74 percent of Americans believe same-sex marriage should be a guaranteed right while 13 percent disagreed and 13 percent were uncertain. A May 2022 Gallup poll found that 71 percent of Americans supported same-sex marriage, while 28 percent were against. "Public Opinion of Same-Sex Marriage in the United States."

(which had governed reproductive rights for nearly half a century).[92] Yet in polling conducted by Gallup about a year after *Dobbs* was decided, only 13 percent of respondents felt that abortion should be illegal in all circumstances, whereas 34 percent thought it should be legal in all circumstances, and another 51 percent said it should be legal under certain conditions.[93]

So, too, with LGBTQ rights. Many felt the issue had been settled in 2015 when the Supreme Court upheld the right of same sex couples to marry.[94] Such thinking may have been premature. Justice Clarence Thomas stated that, based on the understanding of the Fourteenth Amendment Due Process Clause set forth in *Dobbs*, he would, if given the chance, reconsider and overrule "all of this Court's substantive due process precedents, including *Griswold*, *Lawrence*, and *Obergefell*."[95]

More telling perhaps was the Court's decision in 2018 involving a Colorado bakery.[96] The Court ruled that the Colorado Civil Rights Commission did not employ religious neutrality when it found that the bakery had discriminated against a gay couple by refusing to design a custom wedding based on the owner's religious beliefs. The Court specifically held that the Commission's actions violated the bakery owner's rights to free exercise, and it reversed the Commission's decision. LGBTQ activists were concerned by this decision, fearing that it could offer a legal defense to other businesses (such as caterers, florists, or photographers) that refuse to offer services to same-sex couples due to religious objections to same-sex marriage.

Finally, it is impossible to ignore the increase in attacks on transgender rights occurring at the state level.[97] In the first three months of 2024

92. McCann and Walker, "Tracking Abortion Bans Across the Country."
93. The Gallup Organization, "Where Do American Stand on Abortion?"
94. *Obergefell v. Hodges*, 576 U.S. 644 (2015).
95. *Griswold* addressed a woman's right to privacy. *Lawrence* ruled that a *Texas* statute banning homosexual acts between consenting adults was unconstitutional. *Obergefell* held that the Fourteenth Amendment requires states to license and recognize same-sex marriage.
96. *Masterpiece Cakeshop v. Colorado Civil Rights Commission*, 584 U.S. ___ (2018).
97. Examples of transgender rights include protecting transgender employees from employment discrimination (*Bostock v. Clayton County, Georgia*, 590 U.S. ___, 140 S.) Most states allow updating gender identity on birth certificates and driver's licenses, although some require proof of gender-affirming surgery or prohibit updating these fields altogether. Some states legally recognize non-binary citizens, and offer an "X" marker on identification documents. Gender self-identification (including an "X" option) is permitted for passports. In March 2023, Senator Edward J. Markey (D-Mass.)

alone, 523 bills were introduced in forty-one states seeking to block trans people from receiving certain healthcare services and legal recognition. Of these, ten passed. Another 426 remain active.[98]

How does the American public feel about these Court decisions and state legislative efforts? Probably not very supportive. According to the most recent PPPI American Values Atlas,[99] eight in ten Americans (80 percent) favor laws that would protect gay, lesbian, bisexual, and transgender people against discrimination in jobs, public accommodations, and housing. This includes 48% who *strongly* support such laws. Support for these protections has increased over the past few years: around seven in ten Americans favored nondiscrimination provisions in 2015 (71 percent), 2017 (70 percent), 2018 (69 percent), and 2019 (72 percent), before rising to 76 percent in 2020 and 79 percent in 2021. It is noteworthy that this support crosses political lines: overwhelming shares of Democrats (90 percent) and independents (82 percent), as well as two-thirds of Republicans (66 percent), favor nondiscrimination provisions for LGBTQ people.[100]

All this stands in sharp contract with the focus of our third case study: assisted suicide, or as some refer to it, physician-assisted suicide.[101]

---

and Representative Pramila Jayapal (WA-07) introduced the *Transgender Bill of Rights*, a landmark resolution to recognize the federal government's duty in protecting and codifying the rights of transgender and nonbinary people, as well as to ensure trans people have access to medical care, shelter, safety, and economic security. If passed, the resolution would create a comprehensive framework for these protections to ensure that trans and nonbinary Americans are not discriminated against on the basis of gender identity or expression.

98. Trans Legislation Tracker, "2024 Anti-Trans Bills Tracker." These are in addition to the thirty-seven bills that were introduced at the federal level in 2023 across categories such as healthcare, student athletics, the military, incarceration, and education.

99. The American Values Atlas (AVA) is a dynamic interactive online map of the United States' cultural landscape. The AVA draws upon data from more than 100,000 bilingual telephone interviews conducted among a random sample of Americans, with 40,000 interviews each year on political and cultural issue areas. Because of its large sample size, the American Values Atlas allows analysis of specific census regions, all fifty states, and even thirty major metropolitan areas, while providing a rare portrait of smaller religious communities and ethnic groups. See "Nondiscrimination Protections for LGBTQ People."

100. HRC Staff, "ICYMI: New Data Shows Support for LGBTQ+ Rights Reaches Highest Rates Ever Recorded."

101. In the United States, physician-assisted suicide has always been carefully distinguished from euthanasia. Euthanasia, also called mercy killing, refers to the administration of a lethal medication to an incurably suffering patient. It may be voluntary (the patient requests it) or involuntary. Euthanasia is illegal in the United States, but voluntary

Case Studies

The debates surrounding assisted suicide are not new. In fact, in the early 1900s, advocates argued forcefully for legalizing euthanasia, which was already being secretly practiced in the US. The eugenics movement strongly influenced discourse on euthanasia, and opponents of legalization tended to put forth practical rather than religious or moral arguments. When efforts to legalize euthanasia failed, public discourse on the subject waned for many decades until the 1980s, when the pathologist Jacob "Jack" Kevorkian began advertising his services as a "death counselor" in Detroit area newspapers.[102]

Based on a technique practiced by some Dutch physicians, Kevorkian created his own device with which patients could self-administer lethal medications. His first patient ended her life in 1990 while lying on a bed inside Kevorkian's Volkswagen van. He went on to assist with some 130 deaths by suicide over the next eight years. In 1999, after Kevorkian publicly distributed a video of himself directly euthanizing a patient, he was convicted of second-degree murder and sent to prison.

Following Kevorkian's conviction, a groups of physicians filed suit against New York's Attorney General, arguing that the State of New York's prohibition against physician-assisted suicide violated the Equal Protection Clause of the Fourteenth Amendment. The Supreme Court rejected this claim in 1997, ruling that there is no constitutionally-protected right to die.[103] The Court further held that such decisions ought to be left to the states. In a second case that year, the Court ruled that a right to aid in dying was not protected by the Due Process Clause.[104]

Based on these rulings, several states took the initiative. Oregon became the first to pass its death with dignity law that same year. More than a decade later, Washington legalized Physician Aid in Dying (AID) in 2008. Montana decriminalized the practice a year later. Vermont legalized it in 2013. These states, however, were out of step with general public sentiment which was often not supportive of the idea of assisted suicide.

---

euthanasia is legal in Belgium, Colombia, Luxembourg, and Canada. It is decriminalized in the Netherlands.

102. Dugdale, Lerner, and Callahan, "Pros and Cons of Physician Aid in Dying," 747.
103. *Vacco v. Quill*, 521 U.S. 793 (1997).
104. *Washington v. Glucksberg*, 521 U.S. 702 (1997).

DO YOU CONSIDER DOCTOR-ASSISTED SUICIDE MORALLY ACCEPTABLE OR MORALLY WRONG?[105]

Year	Morally Acceptable	Morally Wrong
2001	49%	40%
2002	50%	44%
2003	45%	49%
2004	53%	41%
2005	49%	46%
2006	50%	41%
2007	49%	44%
2008	51%	44%
2009	NA	NA
2010	46%	46%
2011	45%	48%
2012	45%	48%
2013	45%	49%

Things changed, at least in the eyes of the public, in 2014. That year, a young woman named Brittany Maynard was diagnosed with an astrocytoma, an aggressive cancer that can occur in the brain or spinal cord. She was twenty-nine years old and had been married for less than a year. After four months of treatment, she was told that her cancer had returned and was even more aggressive. Although she was given a prognosis of six months to live, doctors prescribed full brain radiation. She was horrified by the side effects associated with this course of action. The hair on her scalp would be singed off, and her scalp would be left covered with first-degree burns. Her quality of life, as she knew it, would be gone. In brief, the recommended treatments would have destroyed the time she had left.[106]

At this point, she decided, in her words, "that death with dignity was the best option for me and my family." She and her husband left California and relocated to Oregon, because Oregon was, at that time, one of only five states where assisted suicide was authorized. In her remaining months (she died on November 1), Maynard became a spokesperson for the legalization

---

105. Statista Research Department, "Americans' Moral Stance Towards Doctor-Assisted Suicide from 2001 to 2023."

106. Maynard, "My right to death with dignity at 29."

Case Studies

of assisted suicide. Her well-publicized death by lethal ingestion in Oregon influenced her home state of California to legalize the procedure in 2015. Today, physician-assisted suicide is legal in eleven jurisdictions.[107]

It is quite possible that the increased legalization of physician-assisted suicide was influenced by people's emotional responses to Maynard's tragic death. It does not, however, address the arguments of those opposed to the procedure. The first of these is best described as "suicide contagion."

The sociologist David Phillips first described suicide contagion in the 1970s. He showed that after high profile suicides, society would witness a broad spike in suicides. This was particularly true for individuals whose demographic profiles were similar to those of the person who died by suicide. This finding was corroborated in 2017 by the spike in youth suicides following the airing of Netflix's *13 Reasons Why*. More on point, publicly-available data from Oregon reveal that in the months surrounding Maynard's high-profile death in November 2014, the number of similarly situated individuals in Oregon who ended their lives by lethal ingestion more than doubled.[108]

A second argument raised by opponents of assisted suicide involves the idea of "a slippery slope." They point to an expanding list of reasons for choosing assisted suicide. Cumulative Oregon data suggest that most assisted suicides are prompted by concerns about "losing autonomy" (90.6 percent) or are "less able to engage in activities making life enjoyable" (89.1 percent). Some fear a "loss of dignity" (74.4 percent); being a "burden on family, friends/caregivers" (44.8 percent); or "losing control of bodily functions" (44.3 percent). Concern about inadequate pain control was the reason for pursuing a lethal ingestion in only 25.7 percent of cases.[109]

---

107. They are as follows: California, Colorado, District of Columbia, Hawaii, Montana, Maine, New Jersey, New Mexico, Oregon, Vermont, and Washington. These laws (excluding Montana since there is no law) expressly state that "actions taken in accordance with [the Act] shall not, for any purpose, constitute suicide, assisted suicide, mercy killing or homicide, under the law." This distinguishes the legal act of "medical aid in dying" from the act of helping someone die by suicide, which is prohibited by statute in forty-two states and prohibited by common law in an additional six states and the District of Columbia. "Assisted Suicide Laws in the United States."

108. Dugdale, Lerner, and Callahan, "Pros and Cons of Physician Aid in Dying," 747–750. It is worth noting that from 1998 (when Oregon started recording data) to 2013, the number of lethal prescriptions written each year increased at a much lower rate, an average of 12.1 percent.

109. Dugdale, Lerner, and Callahan, "Pros and Cons of Physician Aid in Dying," 747–750.

A third objection to assisted suicide is depression. Up to half of patients with cancer suffer from symptoms of depression.[110] The elderly also suffer from high rates of depression and suicide. Because depression often manifests somatically, if patients are not screened, clinicians miss half of all cases of clinical depression. This is consistent with data from Oregon, where more than 70 percent of patients who choose assisted suicide are elderly and have cancer, but fewer than five percent are referred to a psychiatrist or psychologist to rule out clinical depression.[111]

Supporters of assisted suicide have counter arguments for each of these objections. No one knows or can predict which side will ultimately hold sway, but for our purposes, the debate is academic. Today, questions surrounding assisted suicide have been settled legally. The Supreme Court has ruled that there is no constitutionally protected right to die, although, as we have seen in recent years, the Supreme Court considers a precedent to be precedent until it no longer does.

Jewish law is equally settled regarding assisted suicide and has been for centuries. As a general rule, all denominations of Judaism prohibit it and euthanasia as well. Here's why.

Judaism values the sanctify of life above all else, basing this on opening chapter of Genesis: "And God created humankind in the divine image, creating it in the image of God—creating them male and female."[112] This verse led the Talmudic sages to declare:

> Therefore but a single person was created in the world, to teach that if any man has caused a single life to perish from Israel, he is deemed by Scripture as if he had caused a whole world to perish; and anyone who saves a single soul from Israel, he is deemed by Scripture as if he had saved a whole world.[113]

Humankind being created in the image of God further prompted the sages to rule that the obligation to save the life of another person (*pikuach nefesh* in Hebrew) supersedes virtually all the commandments of the Torah except for the prohibitions against idolatry, sexual offenses, and murder.[114]

---

110. Rosenstein, "Depression and end-of-life care for patients with cancer."
111. Dugdale, Lerner, and Callahan, "Pros and Cons of Physician Aid in Dying," 747–750.
112. Genesis 1:27.
113. Mishnah Sanhedrin 4:5.
114. Talmud Bavli Yoma 82a.

Case Studies

Jewish law speaks even more directly to the issue of assisted suicide. The law has a specific term, *goses*, for one who is actively dying. Indeed, one well-known source further refines this term to refer to individuals who lack the strength to cough out the phlegm in their lungs.[115] Yet, despite the approach of death (a *goses* definitionally has seventy-two hours or less to live!), one may not do anything to hasten the death of the individual:

> A dying man is regarded as a living entity in respect of all matters in the world . . . We do not tie up his cheek-bones, or stop up his apertures, or place a metal vessel or anything which chills on his navel. We may not move him, or place him on sand or salt until he dies. We may not close the eyes of a dying man. Whoever touches and moves him is a murderer. For R. Meir used to say: He can be compared to a lamp which is dripping; should a man touch it he extinguishes it. Similarly whoever closes the eyes of a dying man is considered as if he had taken his life.[116]

Maimonides is even stricter, ruling that "whether he killed a healthy person or he killed a sick person close to death, and even if he killed a *goses*, he is executed."[117] Nevertheless, some later authorities backed away from this strict standard, For instance, in a famous passage, the thirteenth-century Rabbi Judah the Pious ruled that one *should* remove obstacles which prevent death.[118] Rabbi Moshe Isserles codified this ruling in his commentary on the authoritative sixteenth-century law code the *Shulchan Aruch*, writing that, "if there is anything which causes a hindrance to the departure of the soul. . .it is permissible to remove [it] from there because there is no act involved, only the removal of the impediment."[119] Rabbi Joseph Karo, the author of the *Shulchan Aruch*, goes even further, holding that it is forbidden to administer medicines to delay death in a terminally ill patient who has a very short time to live and who is in great pain.[120]

The difference here is critical. The basic principles of Jewish law governing end-of-life issues hold that nothing can be done to hasten death.

115. *Kitzur Shulchan Aruch* 194:1.
116. Tractate Semachot 1:1–4.
117. *Mishneh Torah Hilkhot Rotze'ach* 2:7.
118. My Jewish Learning, "Euthanasia: A Jewish View."
119. *Yoreh Deah* 339:1. The examples he gives are the noise of wood being chopped and salt on the tongue, both of which are assumed to prevent the dying process.
120. This opinion as accepted as normative by Rabbi Moshe Feinstein. *Igrot Moshe Choshen Mishpat* 2:73–75. See also Daniel Pollack, ed., *Contrasts in American and Jewish Law*, 15–16.

Between the Laws of God and Man

Nevertheless, hindrances to death can, and perhaps should, be removed. This is a far cry from assisted suicide.[121]

It is here that we conclude our third case study. American law tends to approach the issue from a practical perspective. For Jewish law, questions of theology and morality are the deciding factors. Despite their very different theoretical underpinnings, both judicial systems continue to rule against assisted suicide.

LESSONS LEARNED

In each of cases studies, we see a consistency in Jewish law, meaning, changing societal norms have not brought about changes in normative *halakha*. The Talmudic sages never sanctioned abortion on demand. Yet, they understood that circumstances permitted and sometimes required the termination of a pregnancy. Same-sex relations remain forbidden in traditional Jewish law, despite society's general acceptance of them and despite some efforts to enable LGBTQ individuals to be welcomed members of Orthodox communities. And while Jewish law's position on prolonging life in

---

121. The practicalities and logistics of this are complicated by modern medical technologies that enable doctors to prolong life with medications and machines which facilitate respiration and nutrition. Is withholding medication from a terminally ill patient hastening death or removing a hindrance? What about withdrawing artificial hydration and nutrition? In response, rabbinic authorities express a range of opinions on these matters. Orthodox rabbi Eliezer Waldenberg, for example, does not allow the withholding or withdrawing of any sort of therapy, but he does allow the administration of pain medication, even if that medication could potentially have adverse effects. Conservative rabbi Avraham Reisner permits the withholding of medication and the withdrawal of artificial respiration, but not the withdrawal of artificial hydration and nutrition, such as intravenous and tubal feeding. Elliot Dorff, another Conservative rabbi, allows the withholding of artificial hydration and nutrition as well. In general, Dorff's views on euthanasia are of particular interest, because he believes that the *goses* category is not the most precise legal concept to apply in end-of-life cases. Dorff, in accordance with Jewish bioethicist Daniel Sinclair, suggests that the concept of *terefah* is more appropriate. A *goses* is someone who is in the last hours of life, while a *terefah* is someone who has an incurable disease, but who may still live for a long time. Reform rabbi Peter Knobel sums up how this affects the distinction between a *goses* and *terefah*: "The fundamental concept in the definition of a human terefah is, therefore, the inevitability of death in contrast to the *goses* who is alive in every respect." Ascribing the status of *terefah* to terminally ill patients allows Sinclair and Dorff to arrive at more lenient positions about euthanasia. My Jewish Learning, "Euthanasia: A Jewish View."

Case Studies

all cases may have evolved, assisted suicide (and even more so euthanasia) continue to be beyond the pale.[122]

In contrast, America law has changed (and continues to change) in each area discussed in our case studies. This flexibility is certainly driven by changes in societal norms. In the years leading up to *Roe*, woman demanded great rights and a greater say in their lives, as evidenced by the mantra, "Our bodies! Our choice!" Learning from the examples of the Civil Rights and Women's movements, the LGBTQ community made similar demands for autonomy in their personal lives. However, I believe that there is more at work here. If our premise regarding Justice Holmes's "bad man" model is true, it is not surprising that American law is challenged and often fails in matters of morality. More and more people have come to understand that same-sex marriage does not impact their lives. And if society comes to accept infidelity in marriages (i.e., polygamy) or polyamorous relationships, so what? Is this not a matter of personal choice? Where is the danger to society that laws are instituted to protect us from? Many contend it is improper for the government to consider morality when setting public policy.

There is no doubt that segments of the America population push back on such views. They see legalization of abortion and same-sex marriages as undermining the moral foundations of America. As David Brooks recently observed in an article in *The Atlantic*, "for a large part of its history, America was awash in morally formative institutions."[123] Brooks continues:

> For roughly 150 years after the founding, Americans were obsessed with moral education. In 1788, Noah Webster wrote, "The *virtues* of men are of more consequence to society than their *abilities*; and for this reason, the *heart* should be cultivated with more assiduity than the *head*." The progressive philosopher John Dewey wrote in 1909 that schools teach morality "every moment of the day, five days a week." Hollis Frissell, the president of the Hampton Institute, an early school for African Americans, declared, "Character is the main object of education." As late as 1951, a commission organized by the National Education Association, one of the main teachers' unions, stated that "an unremitting concern for moral and spiritual values continues to be a top priority for education."

---

122. For a detailed discussion of this topic, see Linzer, "Treatment of Terminally Ill Patients According to Jewish Law."

123. Brooks, "How America Got Mean."

Is this true? Should it be true? Who can say for sure, but the post *Dobbs* chaos in the realm of reproductive rights, along with the increasingly bitter fights surrounding transgender rights underscore the problems that inevitably arise when American law attempts to set and mandate standards of morality.

CHAPTER SIX

Final Thoughts

THERE IS LITTLE DOUBT that America's founders were profoundly influenced by the Bible. Yes, we all know the narrative that those who voyaged to the New World were, in part, motivated by a desire to worship as they pleased. What is less known is how the book of Exodus shaped the foundations and development of our country.[1] For example, when the Pilgrims set sail on the Mayflower, they believed themselves to be reliving the Exodus saga. As they saw it, everything they had done for two decades was designed to fulfill their dream of creating "God's New Israel."[2] Thomas Paine was similarly inclined. In *Common Sense*, Paine described King George III as the "sullen tempered pharaoh of England." George Washington, too, was touched by Exodus. In a letter he sent to the members of Congregation Mickve Israel after his election to the presidency,[3] Washington wrote:

> May the same wonder-working Deity, who long since delivered the Hebrews from their Egyptian oppressors, planted them in the promised land, whose providential agency has lately been conspicuous in establishing these United States as an independent nation, still continue to water them with the dews of heaven.[4]

1. I discuss this topic in great length in Travis, *Finding America in Exodus*.
2. Feiler, *America's Prophet*, 8.
3. Congregation Mickve Israel, located in Savannah, Georgia, is one of the oldest synagogues in the United States. It was established in 1735 by a group of mostly Sephardic Jewish immigrants of Spanish-Portuguese extraction who arrived in the new colony from London in 1733.
4. Feiler, *America's Prophet*, 4.

Between the Laws of God and Man

In countless ways, the Bible has had a profound impact on the psyche and culture of America, but not, as we have demonstrated, on its legal system. We like to think that America has consistently opted to put legality ahead of morality in matters of law, and it has, in the criminal justice system.[5] It strikes me that this imbalance, that law trumps morality, has found its ways into many aspects of American life. Think of some of the public debates that have been top of mind over the past several decades and the accompanying demands that laws be passed or changed to address each of these issues:

> Why is it that an individual who is paid the minimum wage cannot support a family, even when working full time?[6]
>
> Why are the costs of prescription drugs so much higher in America than in Canada or in many other countries?[7]
>
> Why do CEOs on average earn 344 times as much as typical workers?[8]
>
> Why do America's wealthiest individuals pay lower tax rates on average than most households?[9]

The list of such questions can go on and on, and for years, they were often deflected by a simple answer. These circumstances are unfortunate, maybe even deplorable, but there is nothing illegal going on.

---

5. This has certainly not been the case in the cultural arena, where for years laws were enacted to govern people's sexuality and reproductive rights based on the morals of society or of state and federal legislators.

6. The federal minimum wage in 2024 is $7.25 an hour. After adjusting for inflation, the federal minimum wage in 2021(a baseline used in many online stories about this topic) is worth nearly 18 percent less than when it was last raised in July 2009. This means that a full-time, year-round worker making the federal minimum wage would only earn about $15,000 per year. Yet, the poverty level in 2021 for a family of two, such as a single mother with one child, was $17,420. Glynn, "Raising the Minimum Wage is Key to Supporting the Breadwinning Mothers who Drive the Economy."

7. In 2022, US prices across all drugs (brands and generics) were nearly 2.78 times as high as prices in the comparison countries. US prices for brand drugs were at least 3.22 times as high as prices in the comparison countries, even after adjustments for estimated US rebates. US Department of Health and Human Services, "Comparing Prescription Drugs in the US and Other Countries: Prices and Availability."

8. Bivens and Kandra, "CEO Pay Slightly Declined in 2022."

9. According to a 2021 White House study, the wealthiest 400 billionaire families in the US paid an average federal individual tax rate of just 8.2 percent. For comparison, the average American taxpayer in the same year paid 13 percent. Oxfam, "Do the Rich Pay Their Fair Share?"

Final Thoughts

In recent years, however, large numbers of Americans, from heads of households to corporate leaders, have begun to push back against situations that are legal but that simply do not seem right or just. Here are but two examples.

In terms of minimum wages, several states have increased theirs beyond the federal level in an attempt to provide workers with a "living wage," including California ($16.00 an hour), Washington ($16.28 an hour), and the District of Columbia ($17.05 an hour). Some high-visibility companies have followed suit, including McDonald's and Starbucks among fast food companies and Bank of America and Wells Fargo in financial services. Other notable examples include Aetna, Walmart, Ikea, and Costco.[10]

The federal government took on the high price of prescription drugs in 2022 when President Biden signed into law the Inflation Reduction Act, which included several provisions to lower prescription drug costs for people with Medicare and reduce drug spending by the federal government (provisions that went into effect beginning in 2023). This legislation also capped the cost of insulin to seniors on Medicare at $35 a month. In his January 2023 State of the Union address, President Biden made clear that his view is that this life-saving benefit should apply to everyone, not just Medicare beneficiaries. In response to that call, Eli Lilly, the largest manufacturer of insulin in the United States, lowered its prices in April 2023 to match the $35 a month threshold.[11]

The reasons why we are seeing calls for social and economic justice being answered more robustly in our times is beyond the scope of this book and, truthfully, beyond my areas of expertise. It would be nice, from my perspective, if Jewish law's emphasis on doing what is just and right played a role in this, but I am fairly certain that it did not.

This is not to suggest that there have been no calls to reform perceived injustices in America's legal system. Often, however, these are derailed by America's partisan and often angry political environment, even when said reforms are achieving their goals. Bail reform is an excellent example, and here is how this narrative is playing out.

---

10. Zitter, "8 Companies Raising the Minimum Wage." The Bank of America example is particularly noteworthy. It has been regularly raising the minimum it pays its employees, starting in 2019. That year it raised its minimum to $17 an hour. In 2020, it went up to $20, then $21 in 2021, $22 in 2022, $23 in 2023, and by 2025, its minimum will be $25 an hour.

11. The White House, "Fact Sheet: President Biden's Cap on the Cost of Insulin Could Benefit Millions of Americans in all 50 States."

Throughout America, those charged with criminal offences, be they felonies or misdemeanors, may be required to pay cash bail in order to secure their freedom.[12] This means that people's ability to leave jail and return home to fight criminal charges leveled against them is typically dependent on their ability to post bail, which, of course, is dependent on their access to money.

Originally, bail was designed to ensure that people return to court to face charges against them, something that is now easily achieved with things like court reminders. Today, according to the American Civil Liberties Union (ACLU), the money bail system has morphed into one that perpetuates widespread wealth-based incarceration. The ACLU maintains that the pretrial incarceration caused by unaffordable bail is the single greatest driver of convictions and is responsible for the ballooning of our nation's jail and prison populations.[13]

The facts seem to support this assertion. Over 60 percent of the people unable to post bail bonds fall within the poorest third of society. Eighty percent fall within the bottom half.[14] This leaves poorer Americans (who are often people of color, thus adding a racial element to the mix[15]) incarcerated in jail awaiting trial, sometimes for months or even years. According to the Vera Institute for Justice, the number of annual jail admissions doubled in the past three decades to 12 million, and the average length of stay increased from fourteen to twenty-three days.[16] Few disagree that the pretrial detention of the legally innocent[17] has been driving prison

---

12. The Eighth Amendment to the United States Constitution states: "Excessive bail shall not be required, nor excessive fines imposed, nor cruel and unusual punishments inflicted." This amendment prohibits the federal government from imposing unduly harsh penalties on criminal defendants, either as the price for obtaining pretrial release or as punishment for crime after conviction.

13. American Civil Liberties Union, "Bail Reform."

14. Rabuy and Kopf, "Detaining the Poor."

15. Rabuy and Kopf, "Detaining the Poor." Unsurprisingly, white men have the highest incomes before incarceration while Black women have the lowest incomes before incarceration. The difference for Black men is particularly dramatic. Black men in jail have a pre-incarceration median income 64 percent lower than that of their non-incarcerated counterparts.

16. American Civil Liberties Union, "Bail Reform."

17. One who is merely charged with a crime enjoys the presumption of innocence as a due process right under the Fifth Amendment, even when being held in pretrial detention.

Final Thoughts

population growth, and a major cause of such detentions is an individual's inability to pay what is typically $10,000 in bail.[18]

Compounding matters are the sheer economics of all this. According to one 2017 study, there are 451,000 Americans behind bars on any given day in pretrial detention, at a cost to local governments nationwide of $13.6 billion.[19] It would thus seem that bail reform is eminently logical and long-overdue, and in fact, reforms are being put in place across the country, including in cities such as Detroit, Philadelphia, and San Francisco, and in several states, including Georgia, Illinois, and New York.

It is important to note that these reforms are, for the most part, working. A November 2020 analysis from the Prison Policy Initiative studied research data from twelve jurisdictions where pretrial amendments had taken place. It found no evidence that crime increased as a result.[20] Yet, one would likely be unaware of these facts from the headlines in local newspapers and many broadcast and internet news reports. Why? Because 2024 is an election year, and coupled with rising crime rates in some areas, bail reform is now at the forefront of longstanding political attacks on criminal justice reform, and changes to the bail system in many states have become a lightning rod for voter apprehensions about crime.[21]

Is this a reflection of the fear, legitimate or otherwise, felt by many voters today? I think so, but I also believe that opposition to judicial reforms such as those involving money bail are rooted in the very nature of America's legal system. Justice Holmes's "bad man" theory has impacted us all, as we have already discussed. It explains why we Americans often and reflexively have a hard time truly believing that convicts and felons can change their ways. We want them locked up, not released with little or no bond to continue wreaking havoc in our cities and communities.

I wish American law, and by extension, America itself, was more embracing of the optimism that underlies Jewish law. Incarceration is not the goal of Jewish law. Repentance is. The Talmud advocates for this when it declares: "In the place where penitents (*baal teshuva*) stand, even the full-fledged righteous (*tzadik gamur*) do not stand."[22] Maimonides ac-

---

18. Rabuy and Kopf, "Detaining the Poor."
19. "Pretrial Detention."
20. Herring, "Releasing People Pretrial Doesn't Harm Public Safety."
21. Griffith, "Bail reform Emerges as New Flashpoint in Midterm Messaging on Crime."
22. Talmud Bavli Berakhot 34b.

cepts this as normative *halakha* in his great legal code.[23] Judaism has always encouraged introspection and repentance. This leads people to think, just as I have repented from my misdeeds, so, too, have my fellow Jews. As a result, Jews tend to view their fellow Jews favorably, even those who may have engaged in improper behavior, for perhaps they, like me, have repented.

Imagine how different America would be today if its citizens embraced such a mindset.

America has been very good to its Jewish citizens. It allows us to openly follow the mandates of our own legal code while we simultaneously respect and adhere to American law. This synergy has led to strong, vibrant Jewish communities across the country. Perhaps at some point in the future, should we face less tumultuous and fearful times, American Jews will be able to reciprocate and infuse the country with a bit of the optimism we feel and experience in Jewish law.

---

23. *Hilchot Teshuva* 7:4. He specifically writes there that: "The level of *Baalei Teshuvah* transcends the level of those who never sinned at all, for they overcome their [evil] inclination more."

Bibliography

Abraham, Abraham. *Nishmat Avraham, Choshen Mishpat*. Rahway: Mesorah, 2003.
Adkins, Judith. "'These People Are Frightened to Death': Congressional Investigations and the Lavender Scare." *Prologue Magazine*. National Archives 48, no. 2 (2016). https://www.archives.gov/publications/prologue/2016/summer/lavender.html.
American Civil Liberties Union. "Bail Reform." https://www.aclu.org/issues/smart-justice/bail-reform.
———. "Fair Sentencing Act." https://www.aclu.org/issues/criminal-law-reform/fair-sentencing-act.
Alexander, Michelle. *The New Jim Crow: Mass Incarceration in the Age of Colorblindness*. New York: New Press, 2010.
"Amendments to the Constitution." https://www.archivesfoundation.org/amendments-u-s-constitution/#.
Aquinas, Thomas. *Summa Theologica, The Treatise on Law*.
Assaf, Simcha ed. *Teshuvot ha-Geʼonim*. Jerusalem, 1942.
"Assisted Suicide Laws in the United States." Patients Rights Council. Last updated January 6, 2017. https://www.patientsrightscouncil.org/site/assisted-suicide-state-laws/.
Berkeley Law. "The Common Law and Civil Law Traditions." https://www.law.berkeley.edu/wp-content/uploads/2017/11/CommonLawCivilLawTraditions.pdf.
Berkowitz, Peter. "The Court, the Constitution, and the Culture of Freedom." Hoover Institution. August 1, 2005. https://www.hoover.org/research/court-constitution-and-culture-freedom.
Bivens, Josh and Jori Kandra. "CEO Pay Slightly Declined in 2022." Economic Policy Institute. September 21, 2023. https://www.epi.org/publication/ceo-pay-in-2022/#.
Black's Law Dictionary, 6th ed. St Paul, West Publishing, 1990.
Blakemore, Erin. "How US Abortion Laws Went from Nonexistent to Acrimonious." *National Geographic*. April 11, 2023. https://www.nationalgeographic.com/history/article/the-complex-early-history-of-abortion-in-the-united-states.
Bloomenthal, Andrew. "Void Contract Definition and What Happens." https://www.investopedia.com/terms/v/void-contract.asp.
Bradley, Joseph. "Law, Its Nature and Office as the Bond and Basis of Civil Society." Introductory Lecture to the Law Department of the University of Pennsylvania, October 1, 1884.

Bibliography

Brander, Kenneth. "Finding a Home in our Midst: Engaging and Welcoming Gay and Lesbian Jews Within the Orthodox Community." https://ots.org.il/finding-a-home-in-our-midst/.

Brody, Robert. *The Geonim of Babylonia and the Shaping of Medieval Jewish Culture*. New Haven: Yale University Press, 2013.

Brooks, David. "How America Got Mean." *The Atlantic*. August 14, 2023. https://www.theatlantic.com/magazine/archive/2023/09/us-culture-moral-education-formation/674765/.

Broyde, Michael J. "Rights and Duties in the Jewish Tradition." In Contrasts in American and Jewish Law. Daniel Pollack, ed. New York: Ktav, 2001.

Broyde, Michael J. and Mark Goldfeder. "The Behavior of Jewish Judges: A Theoretical Study of Religious Decision-making." *Bekhol Derakhekha Daehu* 33 (2018) 63–81.

Broyde, Michael J., and Reuven Travis. *Sex in the Garden: Consensual Encounters Gone Bad*. Eugene: Wipf & Stock, 2019.

———. *Finding America in Exodus: A Blueprint for "A More Perfect Union" in the 21st Century*. Eugene: Wipf & Stock, 2022.

———. *Finding America in Leviticus: Reflections on Nation-Building in the 21st Century*. Eugene: Wipf & Stock, 2023.

Bryant, Erica. "Why Punishing People in Jail and Prison Isn't Working." Vera Institute. October 24, 2023. https://www.vera.org/news/why-punishing-people-in-jail-and-prison-isnt-working#.

Choi, Joseph. "Alabama Supreme Court Rules Frozen Embryos are 'Children.'" *The Hill*. February 19, 2024. https://thehill.com/homenews/state-watch/4477607-alabama-supreme-court-rules-frozen-embryos-are-children/.

Cipriano, Sofia. "The First Amendment and the Abortion Rights Debate." *Princeton Legal Journal*. February 7, 2024. https://legaljournal.princeton.edu/the-first-amendment-and-the-abortion-rights-debate/.

Corwin, Emily P., Robert J. Cramer, Desiree A. Griffin and Stanley L. Brodsky. "Defendant Remorse, Need for Affect, and Juror Sentencing Decisions." *Journal of the American Academy of Psychiatry and the Law* 40, no. 1 (2012) 41–49. PMID: 22396340.

"Courts and Legal Procedure: The Role of Judges." https://www.americanbar.org/groups/public_education/resources/law_related_education_network/how_courts_work/judge_role/.

Czopek, Madison. "US public schools are still teaching about the Declaration of Independence," April 10, 2023. https://www.poynter.org/fact-checking/2023/schools-stop-teaching-declaration-independence/.

Dainow, Joseph. "The Civil Law and the Common Law: Some Points of Comparison." *The American Journal of Comparative Law* 15, no. 3 (1966 - 1967).

Davidson, Jon W. "A Brief History of the Path to Securing LGBTQ Rights." July 5, 2022. https://www.americanbar.org/groups/crsj/publications/human_rights_magazine_home/intersection-of-lgbtq-rights-and-religious-freedom/a-brief-history-of-the-path-to-securing-lgbtq-rights/.

Dilanian, Ken. "Most People Think the US Crime Rate is Rising. They're Wrong." December 16, 2023. *NBC News*. https://www.nbcnews.com/news/us-news/people-think-crime-rate-up-actually-down-rcna129585.

"Dina De-Malkhuta Dina." https://www.jewishvirtuallibrary.org/dina-de-malkhuta-dina.

Downs, Jim. "The Gay Liberation Movement." Bill of Rights Institute. https://billofrightsinstitute.org/essays/the-gay-liberation-movement.

Bibliography

Dudley, Jonathan. "When The 'Biblical View' For Evangelicals Was That Life Begins at Birth." *Religion Dispatches.* September 27, 2019. https://religiondispatches.org/when-the-biblical-view-for-evangelicals-was-that-life-begins-at-birth/.

Dugdale, Lydia S., Barron H. Lerner, and Daniel Callahan. "Pros and Cons of Physician Aid in Dying." *Yale Journal of Biology and Medicine,* 92 (2019) 747–750. https://www.ncbi.nlm.nih.gov/pmc/articles/PMC6913818/.

Echols, Ted N. "Decriminalizing Adultery: An Unanticipated Step in Restoring the Value of Marriage." *Liberty University Law Review* 16, no. 2, (2022). https://digitalcommons.liberty.edu/lu_law_review/vol16/iss2/2.

Eisenberg, Daniel. "Abortion in Jewish Law." Aish. https://aish.com/abortion-in-jewish-law/.

El-Bawab, Nadine, Tess Scott, Christina Ng, and Acacia Nunes. "Delayed and Denied: Women Pushed to Death's Door for Abortion Care in post-Roe America." ABC News. December 14, 2023. https://abcnews.go.com/US/delayed-denied-women-pushed-deaths-door-abortion-care/story?id=105563255.

Elon, Menachem. "Rabbi Isaac Alfasi: Rif, A legal code for the Jews of medieval North Africa and Spain." https://www.myjewishlearning.com/article/rabbi-isaac-alfasi-rif/.

Equal Justice Society. "Intent Doctrine." https://equaljusticesociety.org/law/intentdoctrine/#.

Feder, Yitzhaq. "Terms of Taboo: What Is the Moral Basis for the Sexual Prohibitions?" https://www.thetorah.com//article//terms-of-taboo-what-is-the-moral-basis-for-the-sexual-prohibitions.

Feiler, Bruce. *America's Prophet: Moses and the American Story.* New York: William Morrow, 2009.

Feldman, David M. *Marital Relations, Birth Control, and Abortion in Jewish Law.* New York: Schocken, 1968.

Forman Jr., James. "Racial Critiques of Mass Incarceration: Beyond the New Jim Crow." *New York University Law Review* 87 (2012) 101–146. https://www.ojp.gov/ncjrs/virtual-library/abstracts/racial-critiques-mass-incarceration-beyond-new-jim-crow.

Friedman, Hershey H. "Talmudic Ethics and its Reliance on Values Rather than Rules." July 27, 2018. https://papers.ssrn.com/sol3/papers.cfm?abstract_id=3221295.

Friend, Celeste. "Social Contract Theory." Internet Encyclopedia of Philosophy.

Gerhardt, Michael J. "The Role of Precedent in Constitutional Decisionmaking and Theory." *George Washington Law Review* 60 (1991) 68–159.

Gilmore, Grant. *The Ages of American Law.* New Haven: Yale University Press, 1977.

Glynn, Sarah Jane. "Raising the Minimum Wage is Key to Supporting the Breadwinning Mothers who Drive the Economy." Center for American Progress. February 23, 2021. https://www.americanprogress.org/article/raising-minimum-wage-key-supporting-breadwinning-mothers-drive-economy/.

Gore, D'Angelo, Robert Farley and Lori Robertson. "What Gorsuch, Kavanaugh and Barrett Said About Roe at Confirmation Hearings." May 9, 2022, updated on June 24, 2022. https://www.factcheck.org/2022/05/what-gorsuch-kavanaugh-and-barrett-said-about-roe-at-confirmation-hearings/.

Gordon, Jason. "Types of Judges in State and Federal Judiciary—Explained." https://thebusinessprofessor.com/en_US/criminal-civil-law/types-of-judges-in-state-and-federal-judiciary.

"Government Persecution of the LGBTQ Community is Widespread." Pride & Progress. https://www.prideandprogress.org/years/1950s.

Bibliography

Griffith, Janelle. "Bail reform Emerges as New Flashpoint in Midterm Messaging on Crime." July 16, 2022. *NBC News*. https://www.nbcnews.com/politics/bail-reform-emerges-new-flashpoint-midterm-messaging-crime-rcna35165.

Gurock, Jeffrey. *Orthodox Jews in America*. Bloomington: Indiana University Press, 2009.

Heinemann, Moshe. "Cholov Yisroel: Does a Neshama Good." https://www.star-k.org/articles/articles/1179/cholov-yisrael-does-a-neshama-good/.

Hepler, Reed. "Conservative Judaism: Definition, History & Beliefs." November 21, 2023, https://study.com/learn/lesson/conservative-judaism-beliefs-history.html.

Herring, Tiana. "Releasing People Pretrial Doesn't Harm Public Safety." November 17, 2020. Prison Policy Initiative. https://www.prisonpolicy.org/blog/2020/11/17/pretrial-releases/.

History.com Editors. "Gay Rights." History.com. June 28, 2017, updated June 20, 2024. https://www.history.com/topics/gay-rights/history-of-gay-rights.

"HIV and AIDS—United States, 1981–2000." *Morbidity and Mortality Weekly Report*, June 1, 2001, 50 (21), 430–434, CDC. https://www.cdc.gov/mmwr/preview/mmwrhtml/mm5021a2.htm.

Holland, Jennifer L. "Abolishing Abortion: The History of the Pro-Life Movement in America." Organization of American Historians. https://www.oah.org/tah/november-3/abolishing-abortion-the-history-of-the-pro-life-movement-in-america/.

Holmes, Oliver Wendell. "The Path of the Law." *Harvard Law Review* 10, 457 (1897).

"How COVID-19 Changed Crime in the US." January 27, 2023. Public Affairs, Northeastern University. https://publicaffairs.northeastern.edu/articles/us-crime-rate-during-pandemic/.

HRC Staff, "ICYMI: New Data Shows Support for LGBTQ+ Rights Reaches Highest Rates Ever Recorded." Human Rights Campaign. March 27, 2023. https://www.hrc.org/press-releases/icymi-new-data-shows-support-for-lgbtq-rights-reaches-highest-rates-ever-recorded.

Jacobs, Jill. "What Is Shatnez?" www.myjewishlearning. Com/article/ shatnez/.

Jacobs, Louis. "Joseph Caro: Medieval Lawyer and Mystic." https://www.myjewishlearning.com/article/joseph-caro/.

"Jewish Population Rises to 15.3 Million Worldwide, with Over 7 Million Residing in Israel." https://www.jewishagency.org/jewish-population-rises-to-15-3-million-worldwide-with-over-7-million-residing-in-israel/.

Jewish Virtual Library. "Law of Obligations." https://www.jewishvirtuallibrary.org/obligations-law-of#.

Jimenez, Marco. "Finding the Good in Justice Holmes's Bad Man." *Fordham Law Review* 79, 5 (2011) 2070. http://ir.lawnet.fordham.edu/flr/vol79/iss5/9.

"Justice." University of Texas at Austin. Ethic Unwrapped. https://ethicsunwrapped.utexas.edu/glossary/justice#.

Kellman, Rabbi Jay. "The Law of the Land: Bava Kamma 113." https://torahinmotion.org/discussions-and-blogs/the-law-of-the-land-bava-kamma-113.

Keyes, Oprah. "Mass Incarceration & People of Color, Southern Coalition for Social Justice." https://southerncoalition.org/mass-incarceration-people-color/#_ftn5.

King Jr., Martin Luther. "Letter from a Birmingham Jail." April 16, 1963. https://bri-wp-images.s3.amazonaws.com/wp-content/uploads/Letter-From-Birmingham-Jail.pdf.

Bibliography

Lamanna, Mary Ann, Agnes Riedmann, Susan D. Stewart. *Marriages, Families, and Relationships: Making Choices in a Diverse Society*. Cengage Learning. Belmont: Wadsworth, 2014.

"Laws That Are Made to Be Broken: Adjusting for Anticipated Noncompliance." *Michigan Law Review* 75, no. 4 (1977) 687–716. https://doi.org/10.2307/1287911.

Lee, Thomas. "Civil Law's Influence on American Constitutionalism." https://www.law.nyu.edu/sites/default/files/upload_documents/Lee%20Civil%20Law%20Tradition%20NYU%20Final%20Draft.pdf.

Lepore, Jill. "The Supreme Court's Selective Memory. *The New Yorker*. June 24, 2022. https://www.newyorker.com/news/daily-comment/the-supreme-courts-selective-memory-on-gun-rights.

"Letter from Thomas Jefferson to Isaac H. Tiffany," April 4, 1819. https://founders.archives.gov/documents/Jefferson/03-14-02-0191.

Levine, Samuel J. "Teshuva: A Look at Repentance, Forgiveness And Atonement In Jewish Law And Philosophy And American Legal Thought." https://lessons.myjli.com/crime/index.php/lesson-4/teshuva-a-look-at-repentance-forgiveness-and-atonement-in-jewish-law-and-philosophy-and-american-legal-thought/.

Liptak, Adam. "Supreme Court Says Kentucky Clerk Must Let Gay Couples Marry." *The New York Times*, August 31, 2015.

Linzer, Dov. "Treatment of Terminally Ill Patients According to Jewish Law." *AMA Journal of Ethics* (December 2013). https://journalofethics.ama-assn.org/article/treatment-terminally-ill-patients-according-jewish-law/2013-12.

Locke, John. *The Second Treatise of Civil Government and A Letter Concerning Toleration*. Oxford: B. Blackwell, 1948.

———. *Two Treatises of Government*. England: Phoenix, 1993.

Lloyd, Robert M. "The Reasonable Certainty Requirement in Lost Profits Litigation: What It Really Means." *University of Tennessee Legal Studies Research Paper No. 128* (2010). https://ir.law.utk.edu/cgi/viewcontent.cgi?article=1190&context=transactions.

Lustiger, Arnold, ed. *Chumash Mesoras Harav: Sefer Shemos*. Oklahoma University Press, 2014.

Maimonides *The Guide for the Perplexed*. https://www.sefaria.org/Guide_for_the_Perplexed?tab=contents.

———. Maimonides, *Mishneh Torah*. https://www.sefaria.org/texts/Halakhah/Mishneh%20Torah.

Mayflower Compact. https://themayflowersociety.org/history/the-mayflower-compact/.

"Mass Incarceration & People of Color." Southern Coalition for Social Justice. https://southerncoalition.org/mass-incarceration-people-color/.

Maynard, Brittany. "My Right to Death with Dignity at 29." *CNN*. November 2, 2014. https://www.cnn.com/2014/10/07/opinion/maynard-assisted-suicide-cancer-dignity/index.html.

Mbewe, Seman. "The role of law." World Development Report. The World Bank, 2017. https://openknowledge.worldbank.org/server/api/core/bitstreams/b52bc50a-a10c-5f2f-9c0f-5bd5dab99f25/content.

McCann, Allison and Amy Schoenfeld Walker. "Tracking Abortion Bans Across the Country," *The New York Times*. January 8, 2024. https://www.nytimes.com/interactive/2022/us/abortion-laws-roe-v-wade.html.

Melamed, Eliezer. "Regarding LGBT—Education and Love." *B'Sheva*. August 2, 2018. https://tinyurl.com/melamed-lgbt.

Bibliography

My Jewish Learning. "Text of Kol Nidre." https://www.myjewishlearning.com/article/text-of-kol-nidre//.

———. "Moshe Feinstein." https://www.myjewishlearning.com/article/moshe-feinstein/.

———. "Abortion and Judaism." https://www.myjewishlearning.com/article/abortion-in-jewish-thought/.

———. "Euthanasia: A Jewish View." https://www.myjewishlearning.com/article/euthanasia-a-jewish-view/.

———. "The World to Come." https://www.myjewishlearning.com/article/the-world-to-come/.

"Narrative Shift and The Campaign to End Racial Profiling." The Opportunity Agenda, 2022. https://opportunityagenda.org/messaging_reports/shifting-the-narrative/case-6/.

National Research Council. *The Growth of Incarceration in the United States: Exploring Causes and Consequences.* Washington, DC: The National Academies Press, 2014. https://doi.org/10.17226/18613.

"Natural Law, Human Rights, and Unalienable Rights: A Canopy Forum Thematic Series," January 2020. https://canopyforum.org/natural-law-human-rights-and-unalienable-rights/.

Ngun TC and E. Vilain. "The Biological Basis of Human Sexual Orientation: Is There a Role for Epigenetics? *Adv Genet* 86 (2014) 167–84. doi: 10.1016/B978-0-12-800222-3.00008-5. PMID: 25172350.

"Nine States Have Reduced Their Prisoner Population by 30%. What Do They Have in Common?" *Criminon International.* October 12, 2023. https://www.criminon.org/who-we-are/groups/criminon-international/nine-states-have-reduced-their-prisoner-population-by-30-percent/#fn:5.

"Nondiscrimination Protections for LGBTQ People." PRRI, 2018. https://www.prri.org/american-values-atlas/.

OU Staff, "Tefach." https://www.ou.org/judaism-101/glossary/tefach/#.

Oxfam. "Do the Rich Pay Their Fair Share?" January 14, 2024. https://www.oxfamamerica.org/explore/stories/do-the-rich-pay-their-fair-share/.

Potter, Doug. "Five Reasons Abortion is Murder: The Killing of an Innocent Human Being." October 28, 2022. https://ses.edu/five-reasons-abortion-is-murder-the-killing-of-an-innocent-human-being/.

Pew Research Center. "A Portrait of Jewish Americans." October 1, 2013. https://www.pewresearch.org/religion/2013/10/01/jewish-american-beliefs-attitudes-culture-survey/.

———. "Jewish American in 2020." "Jewish Practices and Customs." May 11, 2021. https://www.pewresearch.org/religion/2021/05/11/jewish-practices-and-customs/.

Pollack, Daniel, ed. *Contrasts in American and Jewish Law.* New York: Yeshiva University Press, 2001.

"Pretrial Detention." Prison Policy Initiative. https://www.prisonpolicy.org/research/pretrial_detention/.

"Public Opinion of Same-Sex Marriage in the United States." Wikipedia.com. https://en.wikipedia.org/wiki/Public_opinion_of_same-sex_marriage_in_the_United_States.

Rabuy, Bernadette and Daniel Kopf. "Detaining the Poor: How Money Bail Perpetuates an Endless Cycle of Poverty and Jail Time." May 10, 2016. Prison Policy Initiative. https://www.prisonpolicy.org/reports/incomejails.html.

Bibliography

Rinehart, Stephen. "Proving Intentional Discrimination in Equal Protection Cases: The Growing Burden of Proof in the Supreme Court." *N.Y.U. Review of Law & Social Change* 10, no. 3. https://socialchangenyu.com/wp-content/uploads/2017/12/Stephen-Rinehart_RLSC_10.3.pdf.

Reardon, David C. "The Abortion and Mental Health Controversy: A Comprehensive Literature Review of Common Ground Agreements, Disagreements, Actionable Recommendations, and Research Opportunities." *SAGE Open Med.* 6. October 29, 2018.

Reiss, Yona. "Camels, Cows and Chalav Certification." *Journal of Halacha and Contemporary Society LLX.* https://consumer.crckosher.org/publications/camels-cows-and-chalav-certification/#_ftn29.

Riga, Peter J. "The Law and Morals: The Perennial and Necessary Tandem." https://digitalcommons.law.seattleu.edu/cgi/viewcontent.cgi?article=1093&context=sulr.

Rosenberg, Jason. "Can a Reform Jew Believe the Torah is the Word of God?" https://reformjudaism.org/learning/answers-jewish-questions/can-reform-jew-believe-torah-word-god.

Rosenfeld, Dovid. "Ashkenazi vs Sephardic Jews: Their Differences & Origins." https://aish.com/ashkenazi-versus-sephardic-jews/.

Rosenstein, DL. "Depression and End-of-Life Care for Patients with Cancer." *Dialogues in Clinical Neuroscience* 13, no. 1 (2011) 101–8. https://www.ncbi.nlm.nih.gov/pmc/articles/PMC3181973/.

Rosensweig, Itamar. "The Legal Philosophy and Jurisprudence of Rabbi Moshe ben Nahman (Ramban)." PhD diss., Yeshiva University, 2022.

Ryman, Hana M. and J. Mark Alcorn. "Establishment Clause: Separation of Church and State." Free Speech Center at Middle Tennessee State University. October 17, 2023, updated on July 23, 2024. https://firstamendment.mtsu.edu/article/establishment-clause-separation-of-church-and-state/.

Saiman, Chaim N. *Halakhah: The Rabbinic Idea of Law.* Princeton: Princeton University Press, 2018.

Santa Cruz, Jamie. "Rethinking Prison as a Deterrent to Future Crime." JSTOR Daily. July 18, 2022. https://daily.jstor.org/rethinking-prison-as-a-deterrent-to-future-crime/.

Segall, Eric. "An Originalism Scorecard Since Justice Barrett Arrived on the Court: Living Constitutionalism is Way Ahead." December 20, 2023. https://www.dorfonlaw.org/2023/12/an-originalism-scorecard-since-justice.html.

Segers, Grace. "The Language of Abortion Is Going Through a Seismic Overhaul." *The New Republic.* September 25, 2023. https://newrepublic.com/article/175712/language-abortion-going-seismic-overhaul.

Statista Research Department. "Americans' Moral Stance Towards Doctor-Assisted Suicide from 2001 to 2023." Statista.com. April 5, 2024. https://www.statista.com/statistics/225938/americans-moral-stance-towards-doctor-assisted-suicide/.

The Chumash: The Stone Edition. Mesorah Publication Ltd., 1993.

The Gallup Organization. "Where Do American Stand on Abortion?" June 17, 2024. https://news.gallup.com/poll/321143/americans-stand-abortion.aspx.

"The Laws of Lo Plug." https://halakha2go.com/?number=665.

"The Prison Paradox: More Incarceration Will Not Make Us Safer." National Institute of Corrections, 2017. https://nicic.gov/weblink/prison-paradox-more-incarceration-will-not-make-us-safer-2017

"The Role of Judges." https://naacp.org/find-resources/know-your-rights/role-judges#.

Bibliography

The White House. "Fact Sheet: President Biden's Cap on the Cost of Insulin Could Benefit Millions of Americans in all 50 States." March 2, 2023. https://www.whitehouse.gov/briefing-room/statements-releases/2023/03/02/fact-sheet-president-bidens-cap-on-the-cost-of-insulin-could-benefit-millions-of-americans-in-all-50-states/.

The World Factbook. "Field listing - Legal system." https://www.cia.gov/the-world-factbook/about/archives/2021/field/legal-system/.

"Thurgood Marshall." https://www.naacpldf.org/about-us/history/thurgood-marshall/.

"Tort." Cornell Law School. Legal Information Institute. https://www.law.cornell.edu/wex/tort.

Trans Legislation Tracker. "2024 Anti-Trans Bills Tracker." https://translegislation.com.

Understanding Stare Decisis. December 16, 2022. https://www.americanbar.org/groups/public_education/publications/preview_home/understand-stare-decisis/.

US Congress, House of Representatives, Committee on the Judiciary, *Defense of Marriage Act*. 104th Congress, 2nd Session, 1996, H. Report. 104-664.

US Department of Health and Human Services. "Comparing Prescription Drugs in the US and Other Countries: Prices and Availability." Assistant Secretary for Planning and Evaluation. January 31, 2024.

US News, "A Former Clerk Who Refused to Issue Marriage Licenses Must Pay $260,000 in Fees and Costs, a Judge Rules." January 2, 2024. https://apnews.com/article/kim-davis-marriage-licenses-rowan-county-b99cdf7b93a1e144fdff2c3b24d96c2c#.

Varney, Sarah. "'When Does Life Begin?' As State Laws Define It, Science, Politics, and Religion Clash." August 27, 2022. *NPR*. https://www.npr.org/SECTIONS/HEALTH-SHOTS/2022/08/27/1119684376/WHEN-DOES-LIFE-BEGIN-AS-STATE-LAWS-DEFINE-IT-SCIENCE-POLITICS-AND-RELIGION-CLASH

Widra, Emily. "Ten Statistics About the Scale and Impact of Mass Incarceration in the U.S. A Curated List of Some of the Most Useful Statistics to Help the Public Comprehend the Magnitude of Criminalization in the U.S." October 24, 2023. https://www.prisonpolicy.org/blog/2023/10/24/ten-statistics/.

Williams, Daniel K. "The Partisan Trajectory of the American Pro-Life Movement: How a Liberal Catholic Campaign Became a Conservative Evangelical Cause." *Religions* 6 (2015) 451–475. https://www.mdpi.com/2077-1444/6/2/451.

Zitter, Leah. "8 Companies Raising the Minimum Wage." January 3, 2024. https://www.investopedia.com/articles/markets-economy/081416/top-8-companies-raising-minimum-wage-mcd-sbux.asp.

www.ingramcontent.com/pod-product-compliance
Lightning Source LLC
Chambersburg PA
CBHW071220160426
43196CB00012B/2353